TRANS
FORMA
TIONS

BELL TOWER

NEW YORK

TRANS FORMA TIONS

AWAKENING TO THE SACRED IN OURSELVES

TRACY COCHRAN AND JEFF ZALESKI

Published by Bell Tower, an imprint of Harmony Books,
a division of Crown Publishers, Inc., 201 East 50th Street,
New York, New York 10022. Member of the
Crown Publishing Group.

Random House, Inc. New York, Toronto, London,
Sydney, Auckland

Bell Tower and colophon are trademarks of
Crown Publishers, Inc.

Manufactured in the United States of America

Design by Nancy Kenmore

Library of Congress Cataloging-in-Publication Data

Cochran, Tracy.
Transformations : awakening to the sacred in ourselves / Tracy
Cochran and Jeff Zaleski.
Includes bibliographical references.
1. Experience (Religion)   2. Spiritual life.   3. Spiritual
biography.   I. Zaleski, Jeffrey P.   II. Title.
BL53.C59   1995
291.4′2—dc20   95-24208
                                                          CIP

ISBN 0-517-70150-2

10 9 8 7 6 5 4 3 2 1

First Edition

FOR OUR PARENTS

VERA F. COCHRAN

PAUL B. COCHRAN

JEAN BUSUTTIL ZALESKI

THADDEUS PETER ZALESKI

CONTENTS

ACKNOWLEDGMENTS

Many people contributed to the writing of this book. We thank Carol Zaleski, William Segal, Larry Dossey, Joseph Goldstein, Lex Hixon, Stacy Horn and the members of ECHO, Donald and Nancy Newlove, Miranda Shaw, Taitetso Unno, Simon Verity, Larry Swimmer, William Turgeon, Father Benedict Groeschel, Margot Torres, Father Mina Yanni, and Sandra Zimdars-Swartz. We're grateful as well for the help provided by Martha Maggos, and for the support of Jean Zaleski, Paul and Vera Cochran, Philip and John Zaleski, Aly Sujo, Sybil Steinberg, Helen Tworkov, and Paul Burholt. Thanks, too, to Margaret Flinsch, Paul Reynard, and Stephen and Anne Marie Grant, and to our editor, Toinette Lippe, and our agent, Wendy Schmalz. Last on the list but first in our hearts, we thank our daughter, Alexandra Haven Zaleski.

TRANS
FORMA
TIONS

T RACY'S S TORY

I ONCE HEARD THAT BRUCE LEE KNEW HOW TO STRIKE A
blow that didn't kill at once. It set up a vibration that lived
undetected inside the body, burrowing through some vital
organ until the victim dropped dead years later. One No-
vember night in Manhattan a dozen years ago, I had an experience that worked its way through my heart and my mind
like that blow. In the midst of getting mugged on the streets
of Hell's Kitchen, something happened that transformed my
sense of my possibilities as a human being, and my sense of
connection to the cosmos—and to the divine. The spiritual
life, I learned, isn't a metaphor or a remote possibility. It is a
reality, a way of being in the world, and it is as full of adventure as anything I could wish for in my ordinary life.

As the door of the little Spanish market on the corner of
West 35th Street and Ninth Avenue shut behind me, the
wind blasting in from the Hudson cut through my sweater
and plastered my jeans stiff against my legs. The grocery was
the only pocket of light and warmth this far west in Hell's
Kitchen. All the big Greek markets and little Italian and Arab
restaurants on Ninth Avenue closed down by ten, so for
blocks to the west there was nothing but deserted streets that
led to the crumbling docks that jutted into the river.

The block ahead was a stretch of gutted buildings and

gaps and stands of working-class tenements. I was making my way to my friend Gary's apartment to have dinner, and as I walked I kept my head down, trying to take in as little of the desolation as possible. A typically underpaid young book editor at a major publisher, Gary had moved to this neighborhood because he had been offered a vast amount of space for a small rent. Some days, I saw a kind of lonely urban romance in these streets: Edward Hopper might have painted here. But after dark, I felt vulnerable, though I never admitted to being frightened. That night, I clutched a brown paper grocery bag like a shield against the wind but I still felt exposed, as if the protective sheath around my nerves was missing so that everything was coming in too raw. I worried that I might be getting the flu, and I wanted to be back in my cozy studio apartment on the Upper West Side.

I was pep talking myself past the empty parking lot near Tenth Avenue when three men rushed out at me from the shadows of a gutted tenement across the street. I heard and felt them pounding toward me in the dark before I saw them, and from their speed and intensity I knew that they were predators. They breezed by me, stopped, wheeled around, and took up stations around me, surrounding me like lions singling out a weak calf.

We stood and stared at each other. Incredibly, I was gripped by an impulse to smile and make friends, to defuse the situation by finding common ground. But within seconds I realized that I wasn't going to disarm these men by chatting about the wind. Their eyes were as dead as the bashed-out windows in the building across the street. Victims weren't meant to get a grip on eyes like that.

Two of the three were lanky, wraithlike teenagers, lost boys. They wore the standard urban mugger camouflage of dark hooded sweatshirts and dark baggy jeans. The third was

2

a decade older and as big as a pro wrestler. His faded green sweatshirt pulled taut across his chest and his wrists dangled out of the sleeves. His broad face was all business.

My mind fought off the idea that they would hurt me. I thought about how I would describe the encounter to Gary over dinner. This would take its place as just another tale of life in the big city.

The big guy, the leader, darted behind me and jerked his arm around my throat. I felt his chest heave and heard the rasping of his breathing. Staring up at the side of his face, I saw a long, shiny scar. It was strange to be pulled so close, and it may have been the intimacy that caused me to feel a pang of compassion for him, for the wounding that had made the scar. He pulled his arm tighter against my neck. He was pumped up, panicked, out of his mind.

"Money," he croaked, choking himself on rage. But he was pressing down on some nerve point in my shoulder that paralyzed my arm, and with his arm around my throat I was unable to speak, unable to tell him that I couldn't reach my money.

"Money!"

My vision went black around the edges. I kept flashing on how absurd it was. I couldn't get the money if he wouldn't let me go, but he wouldn't let me go unless I gave him the money.

"Money now!" he repeated like a robot.

My brain started to race, calculating and considering as if it had switched into emergency survival mode. I watched it with detached awe, as if it were a computer, wholly apart from me. Within a few moments, the computer recognized its utter uselessness and crashed, and as it went down I became aware that there was an unusual kind of attention—a light—welling up in the back of my brain.

It was as if an attention that is always in the background of my awareness was coming to the foreground—as if the clouds of my ordinary thoughts and emotions had parted to reveal the sky. This "sky" attention was an embracing, watchful light that filled my mind and allowed me to see myself just as I was—trapped, gasping, all my thoughts and feelings scared away. It filled my body, too, allowing me to experience myself as a whole.

I'd encountered moments of this attention before, in meditation, but this attention had force and direction. It grew brighter until a stream of dazzling white light shot out of the top of my head, soaring up until it was thirty or forty feet above me and about ten feet in front of me, where it merged with a greater light that seemed to come down to meet it.

My body relaxed and the steel arm clamped around my throat loosened its grip a bit.

I realized that I could see myself and my attacker from above. Yet I was still in my body, still rasping and gasping. I could see the top and back of my own head as well as his head, and I could see the two wraiths standing on the pavement. I was dangling from a mugger's arm, knees buckling, looking up at the light, and at the same time I was aware of being part of that light.

As I looked up at this light, this presence, it seemed to gaze down upon me, embracing me in loving attention. I felt buoyed up, completely supported by a sea of love and light, yet I was aware that I was part of that sea. I felt searched, and I was certain that what was being searched for was some feeling that was unknown to me, buried under all the attributes that made me "Tracy." After a time, the light seemed to stop and then pour through a particular spot in the center of my chest. I sensed that the deepest, most hidden corner of my nature was being seen at last. This brought with it an extraordinary sensation of being connected to the cosmos, as if I had been delivered from the prison of my isolation and welcomed to take my place in the living world.

I sank to my knees on the sidewalk. This felt right somehow, as if my body was assuming an archetypal posture of supplication.

An internal voice gave me the message that I would not be harmed, that in a few moments all danger would pass. I trusted that message, and I sensed that the divine presence that looked down upon me with such grave and compassionate concern could read my whole life, past, present, and future, as if it were spread out around me on the sidewalk.

This strange and beautiful communion felt timeless, though it couldn't have lasted for more than a few moments. All the while, I had been slowly, painfully, inching my arm toward my front pocket and the ten-dollar bill I knew was inside. Finally I reached the money and threw it on the ground. My attacker instantly jerked his arm off my throat, scooped up the bill, and ran off with the others.

I had my life back, and as I stared down at the ripped grocery bag, I wondered why the muggers hadn't taken the cigarettes and beer.

What happened to me that night didn't change me all at once. For a long time, I thought of it as a gift, an exquisite anomaly—a near-death experience that had no connection with my ordinary life. It was as if a switch had been thrown and the lead screen of my ordinary thoughts and identifications and automatic reactions had lifted, allowing me to see and sense a world of finer forces, of luminous intelligent energies.

Still, I didn't know how the light had come to me, or why. At that point in my life, I wasn't interested in having a mystical experience. My interest in spiritual work and ideas was focused on finding a way into my life, on learning how to be who I really was. At twenty-eight, I was at a crossroads. Months before, I had left my job as the East Coast story editor for a motion picture company. It was a job that involved having lunch with agents and editors and otherwise chasing books that might have made good movies. I was busy but I felt like a fly buzzing against window glass. I yearned to find my way into the "real world." By the night I was mugged, I was about to move downtown with Jeff, determined to learn how to write because I thought writing could teach me how to open up to life. I thought that writing could take me through the glass into the heart of experience.

Ever since I was a kid in Watertown, New York, I'd been haunted by the hunch that somehow it must be possible to live a richer, deeper, more vibrant life—a more conscious life—right in the midst of my ordinary life. I couldn't have described what I was searching for, but I felt energized and interested whenever I happened to come across a book or an ancient saying that had to do with an expansion of awareness.

In time this undefined search led me to some of the world's great religious ideas and practices. I learned to meditate; I worked with various teachers. Nothing in my reading or my training prepared me for what happened to me on the street in Hell's Kitchen, however. It would be ten years before I learned that there is an esoteric Tibetan Buddhist meditation practice that cultivates the ability to project consciousness out of the top of the head at the time of death. Extraordinary as my experience had been, it seemed so apart from my known universe that I let it sink away into my unconsciousness, where it smoldered like an ember under ash, forgotten but still alive.

In the following years, I tried to meditate and to observe myself in the midst of life, and I had flashes of perceiving the true depth and magic of reality. In those rare moments, I could see the most ordinary things—a chair, a leaf, a thought—just as they were, without reference to their use or relation to me, yet I could also sense the miraculousness of their "is-ness." Their existence, I perceived, was linked to my existence because everything that is, including me, comes from one mysterious source. Still, after nearly fifteen years of spiritual search I felt restless and disappointed and I didn't know why.

One day while I sat at my kitchen table in Brooklyn, looking out the window at the gardens below, the experience with the light blazed up to the surface of my mind. I suddenly realized that what I had lost over the years was a sense of the scale of my possibilities and of the value of my own experience. I had developed a passive, acquisitive attitude toward spiritual work. I had come to believe that the right teacher or the right teaching or tradition could act as a kind of magic wand that would rap me over the head and instantly enable me to see reality in a new way. That day in Brooklyn, it struck me that the most significant aspect of my experience was the knowledge that part of the divine light that had embraced me had come out of *me*. I had seen that in addition to my ordinary self I was connected in some mysterious way to an unknown luminous Self that was an aspect of the divine, or God, or Ultimate Reality. This other Self, it had seemed, was awake and aware in me all the time, even though I was usually completely cut off from it. But I had seen that I could be aware of it, and that awareness hinged on experiencing myself with total openness. I now realized that transformation was an organic potential, a birthright.

The light had shown me that in my essence, I am already linked with the divine. It had reached down and sought out the deepest aspect of my feeling, conveying an immense protective care about my life at the most personal level. I had seen that spiritual transformation isn't a reaching outward, a seeking to add something to ourselves, but an opening up or awakening to a relationship with the sacred that already exists within.

In the months that followed, Jeff and I began to notice more and more accounts of transforming moments, in which people suddenly encounter entirely new visions of themselves and their connection to reality. The conversion of Saul on the road to Damascus, the transformation of Ebenezer Scrooge on Christmas Eve, the revelation of the preciousness of life that came to Dostoyevsky as he awaited execution by order of the czar—these moments and many more, throughout history and across cultures, suggested that the capacity for enlightenment is innate. Transformation— the sudden understanding of one's true nature and place in the cosmos, the apprehension of the great scale of the Self and its inextricable relatedness to the flow of life—was, we saw, something like a seed that cracks open and blooms when just the right pressure is applied. We didn't doubt that, to be sustained, transformation may depend on a map, on contact with an oral spiritual tradition. Yet the stories of transformation that we encountered came to seem like evidence of a secret history of awakening, a current threading through the history of human life.

This current flows through the lives of each of us. Sometimes it is masked by the restless longing for change that permeates our lives and our culture. We want to move, to change jobs, to undergo therapy, to find the right lover—and driving us on is the feeling that some essential meaning, and a sense of belonging to the world, is escaping us.

The teachings of the great religious traditions contain many dramatic tales of spiritual transformation—from the conversion of the disciples upon meeting Jesus to the transformation of the Tibetan Milarepa from murderer to enlightened being. In secular literature, too, we read of moments in which people's understanding suddenly expands: the vision granted one night to the seventeenth-century French philosopher Blaise Pascal, for instance:

> The year of grace 1654, Monday, 23 November, day of St. Clement, Pope and Martyr. From about half-past ten in the evening until about half-past twelve, FIRE. God of Abraham, God of Isaac, God of Jacob, not of the philosophers nor of the Wise. Assurance, joy, assurance, feeling, joy, peace. . . . Just Father, the world has not known thee but I have known thee. Joy, joy, joy, tears of joy[1]

Our attention is nearly always caught by the machinations of our everyday mind—the mind that is constantly judging, comparing, liking, disliking, daydreaming, and weaving great dramas of hope, despair, and revenge from the raw energy of our emotions. Occasionally, though, a shock, a moment of stillness, can free our attention from the suck and drag of habit so that we can glimpse another world, like a beautiful song heard on the radio when the static has disappeared.

> To see, to look at that sky, the glow of it, the beauty of the leaves against that glow, the orange colour, the depth of that colour, the swiftness of that colour—*see* it! To see it you must give your whole attention to it . . . that attention is a living thing, moving and vital.[2]

—J. KRISHNAMURTI

Over time, these moments of clear attention can be as transforming as Pascal's dramatic experience because they carry the impact of a direct contact with reality. When we are really aware, it is as if we are seeing and hearing for the first time, alive and inextricably connected to a living world.

Attention or awareness seems to be a key to awakening to this higher reality, and that is why cultivating attention is an important part of all spiritual disciplines. Here, the painter and writer William Segal describes what it is like to have an awareness that is strong and sensitive enough to embrace the whole of what we are:

> There is a middle ground, a basic Reality embracing self and Self. It may be called my true nature. To discover what prevents me from the experience of it, I have only to look at myself, just as I am.
>
> It is so simple.
>
> At this moment, what is my state?
>
> I let my attention embrace the whole of myself, from the top of the head through the torso, solar plexus, the entire structure.
>
> I am very still in the body. I follow my breath. I watch the movements of thoughts and associations. The feelings become quiet, and the activity in the head diminishes. I am more. I perceive the whole of my world, just as it is.
>
> I remain very still, refusing the mind's inclination to reach for anything.
>
> Thoughts and feelings come and go like floating clouds. They are not me.
>
> The experience is at one and the same time both active and passive. Through sensation of the body, I perceive that I am. Yet, I do not know who or what I am. I am witness to my own existence.

I am aware of a feeling which suffuses the interior of my-self. It is a choiceless, an accepting awareness. With it comes a sensation that extends to and envelops all the parts of the body. I am very still, relating to the silence that is both inside and outside.

Nothing is lacking at this moment.[3]

—WILLIAM SEGAL

DEATH

*And I looked, and behold a pale horse: and his
name that sat on him was Death*[1]

—THE REVELATION OF
ST. JOHN THE DIVINE, 6:8

WHEN TRACY TOLD ME WHAT HAPPENED DURING THE MUG-
ging, I didn't know what to think. It wasn't that I was unfamiliar with stories of the supernatural or the miraculous. My
shelves at home were crammed with books on religion,
magic, and UFOs, and my work as a literary agent kept me
up-to-date on the latest titles by contemporary mystics and
spiritual guides of all sorts. But as fascinating as these books
were, the stories they told seemed vaguely unreal, akin to the
fantastic tales by H. P. Lovecraft and Stephen King that I also
enjoyed. Never before had a genuine encounter with the
miraculous jumped off the pages and confronted me in the
flesh—at least, not as an adult.

As a child, I knew something about a moment of grace.
My parents raised me Roman Catholic, and I believed everything that the nuns in catechism class taught me. Every Sat-
urday morning I stood in line inside our brick suburban
church, worrying over the sins I'd committed during the
week. If I'd committed a mortal sin, terror would grip me as
I waited on that slow line—terror that before I confessed, I

would die and be thrust into Hell. Like many kids, I feared death and its power to yank me into eternity. Inside the confessional at last, reciting the Act of Contrition on my knees, I always felt great relief and full of hope, as if God had given me a second chance by reaching down with his own hands to wash my soul clean.

Later, after I lost my faith, I still yearned for that radiant moment. At college and in my early twenties, I experimented with psychedelics. I combed libraries searching for The Book—the one that would teach me how to live like a god, without God. I studied Dostoyevsky, memorized Nietzsche, sat up all night reading Byron and Shelley and Keats. At the same time, I stopped worrying about death. Full of ideas and art, friends and lovers, my life seemed too rich to end and certainly wouldn't until I'd grown old, in a future too far away to take seriously.

Eventually I learned to meditate. I sat each morning, marveling at how my mind hopped about like a flea and at how my attention could hop around with it or could ground itself by focusing on my breathing body. But in time these marvels grew familiar and my practice grew routine, what I did in between brushing my teeth and eating breakfast. My craving to reconnect with the incandescent sacredness I'd known in my youth faded; to live life without illusion seemed goal enough.

When Tracy told me about her experience, I felt a stab of loss for the God I'd left behind and I wondered if I'd missed the spiritual boat. But I didn't wonder too long or hard, or too often after that. Still young, I figured that I had plenty of time left to sort it all out. As more years passed, Tracy and I married, she gave birth to our daughter, we moved to Brooklyn, and I busied myself with making a living.

Then, in 1991, my father died.

I'd grown close to my father during the ten years before his death. After retiring from his job with the Navy, he'd moved to a one-bedroom apartment in Stuyvesant Town, a sprawling residential complex a few blocks north of our apartment in the East Village and almost directly across Manhattan from my mother's place. I saw him at least twice a month, usually on Sunday morning for scrambled eggs at a local Russian or Polish diner, sometimes just to spend an hour in the park. I can still see him sitting next to me on the park bench, his white hair sticking out in long wisps from the back of his cap, his blue eyes taking in the passing scene as he emphasized one point or another with a wave of his big bony hands.

He was diagnosed with colon cancer in late 1989, and it soon became clear that he didn't have long to live. I accepted his approaching death with what I thought was admirable calm, gratified to know that he would die at home, surrounded by his books and records. Death comes to everyone, I reasoned. There's nothing to be done about it; let me spend the rest of my time with him as best I can. And I did.

On February 28, 1991, as my father lay close to death, I walked with my mother under a dirty gray sky to several downtown funeral parlors, looking at coffins, talking to the directors. We left the last parlor as night fell and went to my father's building. When I pressed the lobby buzzer to let his attendant know we were coming up, a voice choked out, "Something has just happened." My mother and I didn't say a word as we endured the elevator's crawl up to the fourth floor. Released, we rushed to my father's apartment and to his side.

He'd died less than a minute before I had rung from the lobby. Looking at his body lying on his iron bed, his eyes still open but so clearly without life, I felt as if the earth had spun out of orbit. My father's body was there, yet he was not. This could not be; and yet it was, and I knew in that moment that the presence of death was a world apart from the anticipation of it. No reasoning I had done, no plans I had made, had prepared me for the stony truth: that my father, who had carried me upstairs to my bedroom when I was young and too sleepy to walk myself, was gone and was never coming back.

Yet hours later, back in Brooklyn, as I stood at our kitchen window looking at the trees in our backyard, their leaves lifted and pushed by a cold wind, my father's death passed for me from fact into mystery. Without invitation, I sensed his spirit out there among the stars, beginning a journey about which I knew nothing—and about which, no matter how much I read or meditated, I probably would know nothing until the day I myself died. At the same time, with a clarity as sudden as a slap, I sensed the blood coursing through my veins, felt the press of my feet on the floor, watched my breath whiten and curl into the frigid air outside. I felt electrified by the force of life within me, and I realized that although I knew nothing about what death might bring, I now knew something that I hadn't known before: that death is real, and that because it is real, life is real.

> The sole means now for the saving of the beings of the planet Earth would be to implant again into their presences a new organ . . . of such properties that every one of those unfortunates during the process of existence should constantly sense and be cognizant of the inevitability of his own death as well as the death of everyone upon whom his eyes or attention rests.[2]
>
> —G. I. GURDJIEFF,
> *Beelzebub's Tales to His Grandson*

In the months that followed, I thought about these words of the Greek-Armenian spiritual master G. I. Gurdjieff. I came to see that my father's death had entered my being like a hint of the organ Gurdjieff spoke of, and that it was acting upon me as surely as Tracy's experience had acted upon her. Perhaps God will never again reach down to me like He did in my youth, and perhaps the sacred will never announce its presence to me as dramatically as it did to Tracy. Still, because of my father's death, the reality of death, and therefore of life, is no longer conjecture for me but experienced truth.

It seems likely that only an awareness of the reality of death can instill the sincerity and intensity of effort demanded by genuine spiritual work. And of all moments of spiritual rebirth, those midwifed by death may prove the strongest and most vital.

Twenty-five hundred years ago, death—and sickness and old age—taught a young prince named Siddhartha the lesson of his life. Because his father, the king, wanted Siddhartha to live happily and without fear, he decided that his son was to dream the dream of immortality, to spend his years ignorant of disease, old age, and death. So the king decreed that Siddhartha was to live always within the palace walls, in scented gardens and rooms of gold filled with singing birds and beautiful women, and that the sick and dying would have no place on the royal grounds.

When the prince reached manhood, however, curiosity about what lay beyond the palace walls overcame him. Disobeying his father, he arranged to escape through a side gate into an unknown world. Under cover of night, he rode out into life—and found death and decay: a corpse burning on a funeral pyre; a scabrous old man tottering on the edge of the abyss. These encounters shook Siddhartha with such force that he abandoned all desires except one: to escape the world of suffering he had just entered. Pursuing that wish with all his being, he finally achieved enlightenment and became known as the Buddha.

In Christianity, too, death plays the central role. It is Jesus' surrender to his own death, and his resurrection from that death, that forms the central mystery of the faith. In all religions, death stands in an honored position, the éminence grise behind the throne.

Death is the omega of our existence, the vanishing point toward which all our moments rush. Death is the price exacted by life—which always, without exception, is a fatal condition.

The numbers are staggering to consider. According to the National Center for Health Statistics, in the first four years of this decade, over ten million Americans have died. In 1995, more than fifty million people will die around the world, at a rate of nearly one hundred per minute.

Everyone past, present, and future must submit to two cataclysmic transformations: birth and death. Anyone reading this book has one left.

Yet who really understands that they will die? Even those who have encountered the reality of death rarely do, other than in flashes. Despite my father's death, it's only in odd moments that I understand that I will die, and for two reasons.

Above all, I forget what I have learned. It's telling that Gurdjieff emphasized the necessity of a *constant* awareness of death. A worthy aim, but in the rush of life, one nearly impossible to maintain because caught in that rush we forget that the rush will end. Late for an appointment, clipping down the sidewalk through crowds and food vendors and delivery carts, picking up my pace to cross the street before the light turns red, how often do I remember that I will die, perhaps this very second?

Also, even when I remember the reality of death, I rarely have the courage to face it. Death comes to everyone, I know that. Buddha died. Jesus died. My father died. My mother, my brother, my sister and wife and daughter will die. But perhaps *I* am the exception—or, if not, perhaps I can think about it later.

Our denial of death starts early in life. Recently I read to my daughter, Alexandra, *The Story of Babar,* Jean de Brunhoff's classic picture book about the little pachyderm who grows up to be king of the elephants. In the third illustration, Babar is riding happily on his mother's back in the jungle when a hunter appears from behind a bush and fires his rifle. The next picture shows Babar's mother lying on the grass, her eyes closed. Babar stands on top of her, weeping: she is dead.

Alexandra glanced at this picture, lifted her head from my shoulder, and blurted, "She's not really dead. She's only pretending. She's really sleeping." My daughter then tore back the page to hide the tragic scene.

Alexandra has already learned that death is something scary and bad, like wicked witches and too-friendly strangers. The warning signs are everywhere. When she was two, she was first exposed to the way popular culture handles death, through *The Jungle Book,* the Disney cartoon loosely based on the Kipling tales. Near the end of the movie, Baloo, the big friendly bear, dies defending the boy, Mowgli, from a lion. Or at least he seems to die. After a few minutes of lying still, during which his friend the panther memorializes his strength and courage, Baloo opens one eye and basks in the tribute being paid him. He then rises to his feet: a resurrection for the kiddie set. When Alexandra tired of *The Jungle Book,* she fastened on the Disney version of *Beauty and the Beast* and watched with wide eyes as the Beast, presumably killed by his wicked rival, not only came back to life but as a handsome prince to boot. Next it was *Pinocchio,* where she watched the wooden puppet drown, only to be reborn that night as a "real live boy!"

It's not just children's media that finds death so appalling.
The legend emblazoned across the poster for the recent film
version of Anne Rice's *Interview with the Vampire* reads: Drink
From Me and Live Forever. Horror literature, ever popular, is
rife with death-defying immortals: the vampire, the mummy,
the Frankenstein monster, the golem, the headless horseman
haunting the woods forevermore.

Yet beneath their denial of death, many of these films and
stories whisper a secret: Death is the doorway to a new life.
The best of them intimate further: It isn't necessary to walk
through the door to reach that new life; standing on the portal is cause enough. Death *is* fearful, but in its very terribleness
lies its blessing. No writer has captured the twin curse and
promise of death more vividly than Charles Dickens, in *A
Christmas Carol*. In the following passage, Ebenezer Scrooge
has been led by the Ghost of Christmas to Come to sites
around London, including the funeral of an unnamed man
who, like himself, worked long and hard in the financial markets. Now the Ghost has taken Scrooge to a graveyard:

> A churchyard. Here, then, the wretched man whose name
> he had now to learn, lay underneath the ground. It was a wor-
> thy place. Walled in by houses; overrun by grass and weeds, the
> growth of vegetation's death, not life; choked up with too
> much burying; fat with repleted appetite. A worthy place!
>
> The Spirit stood among the graves, and pointed down to
> One. He advanced towards its trembling. The Phantom was
> exactly as it had been, but he dreaded that he saw new
> meaning in its solemn shape.
>
> "Before I draw nearer to that stone to which you point,"
> said Scrooge, "answer me one question. Are these the shad-
> ows of the things that Will be, or are they shadows of things
> that May be, only?"

Still the Ghost pointed downward to the grave by which it stood.

"Men's courses will foreshadow certain ends, to which, if persevered in, they must lead," said Scrooge. "But if the courses are departed from, the ends will change. Say it is thus with what you show me!"

The Spirit was immovable as ever.

Scrooge crept towards it, trembling as he went; and following the finger, read upon the stone of the neglected grave his own name, EBENEZER SCROOGE.

"Am *I* that man who lay upon the bed?" he cried, upon his knees.

The finger pointed from the grave to him, and back again.

"No, Spirit! Oh no, no!"

The finger was still there.

"Spirit!" he cried, tight clutching at its robe, "hear me! I am not the man I was. I will not be the man I must have been but for this intercourse. Why show me this, if I am past all hope!". . .

Holding up his hands in one last prayer to have his fate reversed, he saw an alteration in the Phantom's hood and dress. It shrank, collapsed, and dwindled down into a bedpost.

Yes! and the bedpost was his own. The bed was his own, the room was his own. Best and happiest of all, the Time before him was his own, to make amends in!

"I will live in the Past, the Present, and the Future," Scrooge repeated, as he scrambled out of bed. "The Spirits of all Three shall strive within me. Old Jacob Marley! Heaven, and the Christmas Tree be praised for this! I say it on my knees, old Jacob, on my knees!"

He was so fluttered and so glowing with his good intentions, that his broken voice would scarcely answer to his call. He had been sobbing violently in his conflict with the spirit, and his face was wet with tears. . . .

"I don't know what day of the month it is," said Scrooge. "I don't know how long I've been among the Spirits. I don't know anything. I'm quite a baby. Never mind. I don't care. I'd rather be a baby. Hallo! Whoop! Hallo here!" . . .

Running to the window, he opened it, and put out his head. No fog, no mist; clear, bright, jovial, stirring, cold; cold, piping for the blood to dance to; golden sunlight; heavenly sky; sweet fresh air; merry bells. Oh, glorious. Glorious! . . .

Scrooge was better than his word. He did it all, and infinitely more. . . . He became as good a friend, as good a master, and as good a man, as the good old city knew, or any other good old city, town, or borough, in the good old world.

Before the Phantom shows Scrooge his own grave, London's most notorious miser is a phantom himself, a shadow hunched up against the world, cloaked in suspicion and hatred. Then in a cataclysm of emotion, "his face wet with tears," the knowledge that he will die smashes through him, exposing the childlike soul buried for so long. All spiritual transformations, like Scrooge's, have an emotional content, and no wonder. The sudden awareness that life has been lived encased in psychological armor, cut off from the sacredness of the world, must bring with it a piercing remorse. Rebirth, like birth, is painful: but what follows inevitably is joy.

Fundamental to Scrooge's transformation is a reorientation of his attention. For all his adult life he has been trapped within his frightened self, held hostage to its demand that the world bend to its wishes. But the world bends to no one's wishes—death awaits us all—and those who would bend the world risk breaking their souls in the effort. Scrooge's soul broke and shriveled long before the Ghosts appeared to him, when his beloved sister died. This cannot be, he thought of her death; and yet it was. Anger poured into his heart and curdled into bitterness. In Scrooge, as in everyone, there remained a spark of the divine and a desire to open to it, but in his bitterness he took that spark for the glint of gold. Scrooge made money his God and attended to it alone; and the more he made, the more he needed—and the harder it became to give any of it up.

Left to its own devices, the ego's focus grows ever more narrow until the world is seen as if through the wrong end of a telescope: tiny, controllable, too small to hurt. When the Phantom shows Scrooge his tombstone, however, the shock breaks his attention loose so that it is free to expand and include himself as well as the world. This wider attention remains with Scrooge after his fateful night. No longer trapped within himself he sees the world and himself as they are: "No fog, no mist; clear, bright." He can accept the world and himself without demand, for whatever life brings, he values it for having almost lost it—and for knowing that one day he surely will.

Scrooge's character has altered. Where once he was cruel, he now is kind, generous, laughing. Like a saint, like Buddha, he can't help but be good. Opening to the world, including his own inner world, he has opened up to love.

> Be it life or death, we crave only reality. If we are really dying, let us hear the rattle in our throats and feel cold in the extremities; if we are alive, let us go about our business.
>
> —HENRY DAVID THOREAU,
> *Walden*

Anyone who has brushed death knows the truth of Thoreau's words. It is so often the craving for a clear perception of reality that so often drives people to climb mountains, to hang glide, to hurtle around a racetrack at two hundred miles an hour—to risk their lives in order to fully live them. These experiences can provide moments of clarity that not only transform the present but also the past that the present passes into, by branding the memory forever. No memory bites more deeply than a memory forged during crisis, for in a moment of crisis—dangling by rope and pinion from a great height, hearing of another's death—our perceptions are accompanied by an emotional force that can snuff our daydreams and shock the attention free to see the real world.

In July 1971, in the Bahamas, I experienced just such a moment. My girlfriend and I were living in a tent on an isolated beach on the island of Eleuthera. Each day, to escape the heat, we went skimming in the warm waters offshore. One day—and I remember nothing about this day up to the event I am about to describe—I was wading in waist-deep water about ten yards directly out from our tent while Gwyn swam in deeper water farther along the beach. Suddenly I noticed a shark's fin skimming the surface of the water, heading toward Gwyn. In that instant, the train of thoughts in my head ground to a stop. I became acutely aware of myself standing in the sea, of the clench of my teeth and the cock of my head, of the water dripping down my neck and chin. Today I can still watch the fin, several inches high and black, speeding through the chop. I can feel myself raising my arms, waving at Gwyn, shouting her name. As if caught on film, with my eyes as the camera, I can see the splash of the water ahead of my knees as I churn through the surf toward her. I can see her running to shore—and there the memory fades.

Similar moments of crisis have altered others profoundly. In 1849, six years after Dickens wrote *A Christmas Carol,* another great writer had an encounter with death that brought with it a life-changing plunge into reality. On December twenty-second of that year, Fyodor Dostoyevsky was brought with several others before a firing squad to be executed for alleged subversive activities against the Russian church and state. As he stood in the line of the condemned, every detail of his surroundings took on a fiery intensity— an experience that years later he inserted into *The Idiot.* One minute before the guns were to fire, a carriage raced onto the execution site, delivering a pardon from the czar. Later that day, back in his prison cell, Dostoyevsky wrote a letter to his brother that included these words:

> When I look back at the past and think of all the time I squandered in error and idleness, lacking the knowledge needed to live, when I think of how I sinned against my heart and my soul, then my heart bleeds. Life is a gift, life is happiness, every minute could have been an eternity of happiness! If youth only knew! Now my life will change, now I will be reborn![3]

Our world is filled with Dostoyevskys and Scrooges, men and women who have encountered their own deaths and found their lives transformed for the good. Perhaps most prominent among them are those who have undergone the near-death experience, or NDE. In July 1994, Tracy, Alexandra, and I traveled up to Northampton, Massachusetts, to visit our sister-in-law, Carol Zaleski, an associate professor of religion and biblical literature at Smith College and author of *Otherworld Journeys,* a comparison of contemporary NDEs with those of medieval times. In the house that Carol shares with her husband, Philip, who is my twin brother, and with their young son, John, we sat in a room decorated with icons and a colorful Tibetan *thangka,* or sacred painting, and talked about the extraordinary phenomenon of the near-death experience.

During our conversation, Carol dispelled many of the common beliefs about NDEs, including the idea that a person has to be clinically dead or dying to undergo the experience.

"Some of the richest near-death experiences," Carol explained, "occur in life-threatening situations like during a mountain-climbing accident or while sitting in a car that starts to go off a bridge. These are near-death experiences in which there's no organic cause for the experience other than the fear of dying. The experience is triggered by the sudden impact on your awareness that you're going to die."

Tracy pointed out that, during her mugging, even though she was aware that she might die, her response wasn't the panic she might have expected but instead a serenity and lucidity.

"These people are having a visionary experience, but they don't feel as if their mental faculties are clouded," Carol affirmed. "On the one hand, they're working like finely tuned human machines, able to calculate what course of action they need to take for their survival. On the other hand, they're having a transcendental experience."

But what causes the near-death experience? I'd read newspaper reports of studies that claimed that the experience was, after all, simply a hallucination caused by oxygen deprivation. I asked Carol whether there might not be a simple physiological explanation for the phenomenon.

She nodded. "Sometimes people think an NDE comes about because of diseased conditions of the body, especially the loss of oxygen to the brain. Tracy's experience was typical in terms of the conditions that triggered it. Some popular accounts claim that people who have a near-death experience have actually died and come back to life. They also say that these people are authoritative eyewitness observers of what it's like to die and of what happens after death."

Carol leaned forward in her chair. "In my view, that's totally beside the point. Most people who have NDEs aren't physiologically on the brink of death. It's true that one sort of impairment or another may be involved, and that there may be organic factors at work. The experience can occur under surgery or anesthesia, or during some other state of physiological shock or when there's a loss of oxygen to the brain. But that needn't be the case. The experience is just as likely to happen without those organic factors."

"Then what," I asked, "is at the root of the experience?"

"The key factor," Carol answered, "is suddenly facing the prospect of your own death. When you have a close brush with death, or even a sudden anticipation of death, you're coming face to face with your mortality in a visceral way. And you're dropping the defenses that shield your awareness of death. Normally, we invest a certain amount of energy into denying that we will die. Under certain conditions of shock, that drops away."

Tracy admitted that for years she had kept what had happened to her mostly to herself, as many people who have NDEs initially do.

"These stories sound crazy if they're outside of a context," Carol said. "Now that the experience has been given a name and become a syndrome that people are familiar with, there's less fear of rejection. But even though the experience is known, there's no tradition for it. The experience can't have deep roots or a far reach if there isn't a web of meaning for it, and the whole community has to be providing that. We live in a fragmented culture, which is perhaps why these experiences are more important now than in the past. We're hungry to hear about them.

"Some people," she added, "say that visionary experiences are given to the people who need them, not necessarily to those who merit them. Or that they're given for the sake of the others who will be affected by hearing about the experience. Or that they're given as part of a whole general influx of messages to the culture, not just for the individual. Black Elk made this point about his visions when he said, to paraphrase, that if I had this experience just for myself, it would be meaningless."

Perhaps I and the rest of us who haven't had a near-death experience are "the others" that Carol spoke of. Yet without such an experience, how can we escape the dream of immortality and the denial of death? And even if we can summon up the courage to cast these away, we must still face the forgetfulness that keeps us asleep to our mortality. Is it possible to escape for more than moments from its drowsy grip?

Each of the great religious traditions answers these questions in its own way. In Orthodox Judaism, for example, the *mikveh,* or ritual bath, is generally kept in the same room as the table for *taharah,* the purification of corpses. Buddhism also recommends practices intended to intensify awareness of death and to increase our ability to meet it with equanimity. The more esoteric of these don't sit well with most contemporary men and women—like sleeping in cemeteries and making love to corpses. Other practices involve meditating on the inevitability of death, the unpredictability of its time of arrival, and its certain effects—and to ponder these matters now, before it's too late.

"This I have not done. And this I'm only starting.
And this I'm only halfway through. . . ."
Then is the sudden coming of the Lord of Death,
And oh, the thought will come, Alas, I'm finished.[4]

—SHANTIDEVA,
A Guide to the Bodhisattva's Way of Life

The refusal to accept a time in which we don't exist can extend to the past as well as the future. In his autobiography, *Speak, Memory,* Vladimir Nabokov emphasized not his fear of death but his horror that the world existed before he was born; he found the thought unbearable. Still, most frequently it is the future that we attempt to foil.

I met a traveller from an antique land,
Who said—"Two vast and legless trunks of stone
Stand on the desert. . . . Near them, on the sand,
Half sunk a shattered visage lies. . . .
And on the pedestal, these words appear:
My name is Ozymandias, King of Kings,
Look on my Works, ye Mighty, and despair!
Nothing beside remains. Beyond the decay
Of that colossal Wreck, boundless and bare
The lone and level sands stretch far away."

—PERCY BYSSHE SHELLEY,
Ozymandias

While fear of death may spark a spiritual awakening, it's only another and finer emotion, remorse, that can keep the spirit awake. Remember Scrooge's sobs, his "broken voice," his face "wet with tears." These rackings of the body came not from fear or guilt, each of which serves the ego, but from remorse, which serves the spirit: tremors of an awakened conscience.

Days after my father died, hot with grief, I turned for support to an elderly wise woman I know. I wanted her to tell me that somehow, in some way, my father's spirit lived on, that the essence of the man I had loved was still within my reach. Instead, she told me what I didn't want to hear—that my father was now "beyond the personal." She added that there was something that I could do to help him. She gave me an exercise, one that she had learned from her spiritual teacher, G. I. Gurdjieff, suggesting that each day I picture my father and think of something I had done to cause him to suffer.

The exercise didn't make sense to me and for a long time I resisted doing it. Finally I gave it a try and then another try. I thought of a time when I had shamed my father and of a time when I had let him down. What I found then and later was this: that doing this exercise, I suffered remorse, not only by opening up to the truth that I had caused my father pain but by realizing that *I was powerless to do anything about it.* Stripped of my incessant desire to make things right, I felt vulnerable, without defense, exposed. And while I still don't know how or why this can have helped my father, I do know that in that moment of exposure I felt as alive as I've ever felt—and that the taste of that moment lingers with me still.

LOVE

My place is the Placeless, my trace is the Traceless;
'Tis neither body nor soul, for I belong to the soul
of the Beloved.[1]

—JELALUDDIN RUMI

ONE DECEMBER NIGHT WHILE JEFF WAS OUT, ALEXANDRA and I cuddled on the sofa and watched Walt Disney's *Snow White* build up to that classic moment when the princess is awakened from her deathly trance by "love's first kiss." That night it struck me that this image of awakening has a mythic resonance; it is a pop cultural symbol for our hope that love and the right lover can awaken us from our isolation and welcome us into a new world.

It was fascinating to note how rich in symbols of transformation the Disney movie is. The last scene shows Snow White lying lost to the world in her glass coffin. Great bands of white light pour down from an opening in the forest roof, indicating that divine forces are watching over her and sanctifying her. The message is that Snow White has a special destiny that she will know when she connects with her predestined lover. His touch will awaken a sleeping energy in her that can show her that her true nature, and the nature of all of life, is a creative love. Her childlike protectors, the Seven Dwarves, kneel, weeping and praying around her, but the mood is not of sadness so much as a bittersweet pause. On cue, the prince jumps down from his white horse and delivers the kiss that pulls Snow White back into consciousness and carries her off to a castle in the clouds. That castle and the blandly handsome prince can be interpreted as escapism, but they are also cartoon signs that love can transport us. They affirm that we know innately that experiences like love and sex can bring more than pleasure. At their best, love and sex can be what the German poet Rilke called "a great, an infinite learning"—an initiation that allows us to taste our true connection to the divine.

Anyone who has fallen in love knows its transforming power. In love, we feel suffused by a universal energy that links us to the rest of life. A lover's first kiss really can make us feel like Snow White when she sits up and stretches and is welcomed by dancing bunnies and deer and doting dwarves. We feel that we can see the beauty and uniqueness of reality for the first time. As D. H. Lawrence said in a letter he wrote after eloping to Germany with Frieda Weekley, whom he later married:

> The world is wonderful and beautiful and good beyond one's wildest imagination. Never, never, never could one conceive what love is, beforehand, never. Life *can* be great—quite god-like. It *can* be so. God be thanked I have proved it.[2]

Love is divine madness, said Plato. From the divine heights of love, we can see the sacredness and beauty in our lover's nature and in all of nature. In some extraordinary loves, we can feel as if we are encountering someone we have known before, a soulmate, someone who has been written into the hidden plan of our lives. We can feel transparent to such a lover, seen down to our depths. This sense of recognition and predestination melts through our loneliness and challenges the habitual distinctions we make between inner and outer worlds. Sometimes we may feel so close to our lover that we can taste the mystical bond, the sense of shared soul, that the great Sufi poets described—"apparently two, but one in soul, you and I," as the thirteenth-century Persian mystic Jelaluddin Rumi wrote. Love like this can give us a vision of life as a sacred wholeness. We may sense a divine intelligence behind appearances that can infuse our lives with wisdom, if only we love.

> Love is life. All, everything that I understand, I understand only because I love. Everything is, everything exists, only because I love. Everything is united by it alone. Love is God, and to die means that I, a particle of love, shall return to the general and eternal source.[3]
>
> —LEO TOLSTOY,
> *War and Peace*

The transforming power of love, its ability to lift us out of ourselves and into a new relationship with another and the world, is related to love's cosmic character. When we love, we tap into the great mystery at the heart of the universe. Mathematical cosmologist Brian Swimme points out in his book *The Universe Is a Green Dragon* that love, which he also calls "allurement" or "attraction," is what binds the universe together. "Bring to mind," he suggests, "all the allurements filling the universe, of whatever complexity or order: the allurement we call gravitation, that of electromagnetic interactions, chemical attractors, allurements in the biological and human worlds.[4] If we are able to snap our fingers and make these attractions disappear, Swimme says, "the galaxies would break apart....Galaxies, human families, atoms, ecosystems, all disintegrating immediately as the allurement pervading the universe is shut off."[5]

In love, we tap into this primordial principle of attraction and creativity. We feel creative, moved by the world, and the new lucidity we're granted extends outward toward the world and inward toward ourselves. Love makes dreams, impressions, and memories available to the conscious mind. In love, we can feel as if we're wandering in a kind of enchanted forest, a fertile darkness of dreams and symbols; there, we can encounter our deepest hopes and fears about love and the roots of our attachment.

When love strikes it can feel as otherworldly as a meteor crashing into the earth. It can disrupt all our orderly plans, overpowering our reason and our sense of control. But the great paradox about romantic love is that even as it seems to derange us, it grants us a rare lucidity. Our friends may fear for our sanity when we insist that we can see divine goodness and magic in a perfectly ordinary person, but perhaps we are seeing our lover in the truest light, and that in our deepest nature we *are* full of the love and creativity of the divine.

In James Joyce's *A Portrait of the Artist as a Young Man*, Stephen Daedalus sees the beauty and goodness of all creation in a vision of a young girl standing in water:

> A girl stood before him in midstream, alone and still, gazing out to sea. She seemed like one whom magic had changed into the likeness of a strange and beautiful seabird. Her long slender bare legs were delicate as a crane's and pure save where an emerald trail of seaweed had fashioned itself as a sign upon the flesh....
>
> She was alone and still, gazing out to sea; and when she felt his presence and the worship of his eyes her eyes turned

to him in quiet sufferance of his gaze, without shame or wantonness. Long, long she suffered his gaze and then quietly withdrew her eyes from his and bent them towards the stream, gently stirring the water with her foot hither and thither. The first faint noise of gently moving water broke the silence, low and faint and whispering, faint as the bells of sleep; hither and thither, hither and thither: and a faint flame trembled on her cheek.

—Heavenly God! cried Stephen's soul, in an outburst of profane joy.

He turned away from her suddenly and set off across the strand. His cheeks were aflame; his body was aglow; his limbs were trembling. On and on and on and on he strode, far out over the sands, singing wildly to the sea, crying to greet the advent of the life that had cried to him.[6]

It is not only romantic love that can transform us. The unconditional love of a child can touch us with a sense of the sacredness and the wholeness of life. But if love includes sexual passion, its power can increase exponentially. If we are sexually attracted to the object of our love, we feel charged with energy, and sensitive to the life around us. A profound sexual experience may make us feel as if our body is a house with rooms we've never explored. It is as if we've been huddling in the corner of one tiny room and suddenly doors swing open and lights flick on, and something beckons us to get up and explore. We may feel inhabited—alive in our bodies—as never before.

Sex has its own intelligence. As it strips us down to our essence, it feeds us feelings and perceptions that are extraordinarily fine and quick. Sex shows us that consciousness can adhere to sensation and pass all through the body. A transforming moment, a moment of expanded awareness, seems to depend on an attention that can embrace both body and mind.

In our culture, many who seek spiritual transformation undervalue the role of the body, but most transforming moments involve a heightened sense of the body, of our physical presence here, right now, on the earth. During sex, we can taste the here-nowness of the body. We see that though the mind may wander into the past or future, the body rests in the present—which is why it offers such solid support for spiritual work and is so integral to the practices of meditation and prayer. Experiencing the body in real time, unblocked by shame or shyness or sheer distraction and disuse, can instill in us a deep-rooted confidence in the value and goodness of our life and our human nature. This basic self-respect is an honoring of the sacred in ourselves in the most fundamental way.

Sex is elemental, freeing us from the prison of the mind and of our ordinary emotions. In *Lady Chatterley's Lover*, D. H. Lawrence describes the power of sex to strip us down to our essential self:

> In the short summer night she learnt so much. She would have thought a woman would have died of shame. Instead of which, the shame died. Shame, which is fear: the deep organic shame, the old, old physical fear which crouches in the bodily roots of us, and can only be chased away by the sensual fire, at last it was roused up and routed by the phallic hunt of the man, and she came to the very heart of the jungle of herself. She felt, now, she had come to the real bedrock of her nature, and was essentially shameless. She was her sensual self, naked and unashamed. She felt a triumph,

almost a vainglory. So! That was how it was! That was life! That was how oneself really was! There was nothing left to disguise or be ashamed of. She shared her ultimate naked-ness with a man, another being.[7]

In France, the orgasm is sometimes referred to as "le petit mort," "the little death." Like death, orgasm extinguishes the ego, if only for an instant, exposing our innermost self to the mysterious ground of being: God in the West, the Clear Light in the East. In Tibetan Buddhism, as the Dalai Lama has said, it is believed that a "very gross form" of the Clear Light arises during orgasm.

All the great religious traditions have linked love, sex, and spirituality. God is love, say the poets and mystics of the great theistic religions—Judaism, Christianity, Islam, Hinduism. For them love is the force that drives the dance of life. Love can introduce us to the reality of what Christian and Sufi mystics have called the "Beloved"—that loving presence whom we can meet in the most private level of our own being.

The writing of the great medieval Christian mystic Julian of Norwich expresses this belief that the relationship to the divine is like a lover's relationship to the beloved:

> For when a soul is tempested, troubled and left to herself because of her unrest, then it is time to pray, that she may make herself supple and docile, so as to receive God.... Then we can do no more but behold him and enjoy: with a high and powerful desire to be entirely oned in him, to be received into his dwelling, to enjoy in his loving, to delight in his goodness.... This is wrought, and shall be, by the grace of the Holy Ghost until we die in longing for love. Then shall we all come into our Lord—ourselves clearly knowing, God abundantly having—until we are all endlessly hid in God—him truly seeing and abundantly feeling, him ghostly

hearing and delectably smelling, him all sweetly swal-
lowing.[8]

Unlike the monastic Christian love mystics, practitioners
of Tantric sex actually have sex as a way to come closer to
ultimate reality. Yet in the sacred sexuality that is part of the
Tantric Buddhist tradition, practitioners don't simply abandon themselves to their sexual feelings and abjectly offer
themselves up to the divine. Attentive seeing is the ingredi-
ent that converts sexual passion into a kind of fuel that allows practitioners to experience the bliss of perceiving their
profound interconnection with all things—the bliss of the
experience that Buddhism calls the "realization of emptiness." In Tantra, sexual partners undergo the subtle surrender
of seeing themselves without judgment. By clearly seeing
their identification with sexual passion and other strong
emotions that come up during lovemaking, they begin to be
transformed—to be liberated from the prison of their small
desires and be delivered into a sense of themselves not as a
solid entity but as a spacious awareness that can contain self
and lover and all the feelings that arise during lovemaking.
Tantra is probably the furthest human extension of being
awakened by a kiss.

One rainy autumn day in 1994, the scholar Miranda Shaw
stood in the back of a loftlike lecture room at the New York
Open Center in downtown Manhattan, showing slides of
images of female deities, or "dakinis," as well as of famous
women teachers, or "yoginis," joined in sexual union with
their consorts, their faces alight with delicate, blissful smiles.

"A 'dakini' is literally a 'woman who flies' or a 'sky
dancer,'" said Shaw as she described the dancing, naked
demi-goddesses, draped only in bone ornaments. To those
on the Tantric path, the dakinis are great helpers and de-
stroyers of obstacles, but they are not treated like angels, for

they are unpredictable and untamed. "They have absolute freedom from social constraints, the freedom that comes from knowing reality. Look at them. You can see that they glory in their femaleness and power. They have no shame, zero shame."

Shaw, who has a Ph.D. in Buddhist studies from Harvard University, explained to the thirty or forty people in the room that Tantric Buddhism is a nonmonastic, noncelibate strand of Indian, Himalayan, and Tibetan Buddhist practice that seeks to weave every aspect of daily life and every passion into the path of liberation. As she spoke, she strode back and forth before her audience with the sturdy, stretched-up-tall poise of a dancer, her long blond hair swinging from side to side like a schoolgirl's. Shaw described how her fascination with these untamed women led her to embark on ten years of research, including interviews and fieldwork conducted in India and Nepal over a two-year period. The book that resulted, *Passionate Enlightenment: Women in Tantric Buddhism* (Princeton University Press, 1994), confirmed what many Tantric initiates in the East have always known: that Tantra evolved from insights and rituals practiced by circles of women initiates.

"Tantra was originally a woman's philosophy," said Shaw. "Men were apprenticed to a yogini." She described the way men would track down circles of yoginis, who would meet secretly at night in round temples that were open to the sky. The women would eat meat and drink wine out of skull cups, embracing these forbidden objects in order to get beyond the dualism that distinguishes the sacred from the profane. Blissed out, they would share insights about ultimate reality, as well as secret knowledge about the transforming power of sex.

Yoginis, added Shaw, radiate an indestructible, "diamond-like" confidence and self-respect that does not hinge on the approval of society or on recognition by a loved one. Deep experiences of love and sex give them, and can give us, a sense of living in an embodied world; during sex, we emerge from the two-dimensional world of our thoughts into the three-dimensional world of sensory experience, of embodied life. According to clinical psychologist and University of Chicago researcher Eugene Gendlin, "Not only do you physically live the circumstances around you, but also those you only *think* of in your mind. Your physically felt body is in fact part of a gigantic system of here and other places, now and other times, you and other people—in fact, the whole universe. This sense of being bodily alive in a vast system is the body as it is felt from inside."[9]

Tantra uses sexual passion (along with other strong emotions) as rocket fuel for transformation. The key to the liberation of this energy is a welcoming, nonjudgmental seeing. According to Shaw, followers of Tantra allow their emotions and passions into their meditations, neither repressing them nor acting them out but simply seeing them with a clarity that cuts through the practitioners' identification. Stripped of their egoistic encasements, the emotions are no longer forces that drive us and blind us. They can be experienced as fascinating patterns of energy that can be channeled for conscious purposes.

In order for this transformation of the emotions to occur, Shaw explained, a certain spaciousness has to be created inside a practitioner. Spaciousness has to be maintained between lovers as well, so that they can experience the pleasures of lovemaking without getting swamped and without losing the thread of meditations intended to help them picture their connection with the whole of life. Ultimately, Tantric lovers must learn to separate themselves inwardly from one another even at moments of greatest attachment, because it is only by seeing through the blinding limitations of attachment, by seeing each other "like a mirage in the sky," as Shaw puts it, that they can emerge together into the ultimate reality that is beyond conceptualization.

"The magic kiss!" cried Alexandra during the last scene of *Snow White.* Hopping off the sofa, she threw her stuffed animals in the air, imitating the jubilant dwarves tossing their hats. Looking at her, I felt something tug in my heart. I hoped it wouldn't cost her too much suffering to learn that love, even with exquisite awakening kisses, is not really meant to heal the wounds and cover over the dead places in our lives. Real love is revelatory. It is a force that can show us to ourselves and allow us to taste the possibility that we really are connected with finer energies and higher worlds. But love can consume us; even as we learn to accept love on its own terms, it burns.

> *My love is a fever, longing still*
> *For that which longer nurseth the disease;*
> *Feeding on that which doth preserve the ill,*
> *The uncertain sickly appetite to please.*
> *My reason, the physician to my love,*
> *Angry that his prescriptions are not kept,*
> *Hath left me, and I desperate now approve,*
> *Desire is death, which physic did except.*
> *Past cure I am, now reason is past care,*
> *And frantic-mad with evermore unrest;*
> *My thoughts and my discourse as madmen's are,*
> *At random from the truth vainly express'd;*
> > *For I have sworn thee fair; and thought thee bright,*
> > *Who art black as hell, as dark as night.*
>
> —WILLIAM SHAKESPEARE,
> *Sonnet CXLVII*

If love is to be liberating instead of consuming, we must learn to turn within, to inhabit ourselves as we love, just as Tantric lovers learn to abide in their own awareness in the midst of passion. Ultimately, real love for another is also a deep—and deeply lonely—initiation in seeing who we really are. Real love is always difficult, as the German poet Rilke said, because "it is a high inducement for the individual to ripen, to become something in himself, to become a world, to become a world in himself for the sake of another; it is a great, demanding claim on him, something that chooses him and calls him to vast distances."[10]

Eventually, love forces us to turn within. In the *Symposium,* his meditation on love, Plato called love a child of fullness *and* emptiness, suggesting that there is a kind of desolation built in to every love. There comes a moment in the progress of most loves when lovers feel isolated and unfulfilled, because they have discovered that they cannot find real and enduring meaning by reaching outside themselves, clinging to their lover. They may find that in order to be able to love they must inhabit their own lives, and that it is only by letting go of attachments and sinking into the center of themselves that they can end their loneliness and find in the wellsprings of love and meaning and the connectedness to life that they seek. They may see that it is only by daring to open to the silence at the center of themselves that they can begin to feel the presence of the One whom they have been searching for all along.

This seemingly paradoxical movement of going inward to connect with the world—of going deeper to connect with the higher—seems to be a universal spiritual truth. In *The Gospel According to Thomas,* the anthology of 114 sayings of Jesus that were discovered in a Coptic manuscript unearthed in Egypt in 1945, Jesus is quoted as saying, "When you become acquainted with yourselves, then you will be recognized. And you will understand that it is you who are children of the living father. But if you do not become acquainted with yourselves, then you are in poverty, and it is you who are the poverty."[11]

Love is a mugger, striking without warning and overwhelming us. Trying to meditate or observe ourselves can seem impossible when we are drowning in obsessive thoughts and dreams and emotions. Yet love exposes us. Sooner or later, it sends us into the depths of ourselves to confront our rawest needs and fears, and it is this deep acquaintance with ourselves that many traditions say can transform us. There is a practice in Tibetan Buddhism called Chod, for example, in which personal "demons" are called forth and allowed full play in consciousness so that even the most terrifying fear or addiction or attachment is seen as pure energy after all. If only we could stop resisting and denying, this wisdom holds, the passion that consumes us can yield energy and light. In *The Gospel According to Thomas,* Jesus says, "If you bring forth what is inside you, what you bring forth will save you. If you don't bring forth what is inside you, what you don't bring forth will destroy you."[12]

Sometimes there seems to be a mysterious and powerful connection between the personal and the cosmic. Clearly seeing and accepting some basic truth about ourselves can fill us with a mysterious sense of liberation and reconnection with life. We can feel as if we are in the presence of the Unknown. It is as if a window has been thrown open and the night breeze blows in, reminding us of the unseen vastness of creation. Once when I was complaining that I felt helpless in the face of some dramatic emotion, a friend suggested that I "take the lid off the box."

"Give the dynamite room to explode," he said. "Then it can't do any harm." His advice helped me see that I am not a sealed container that might explode under the pressure of strong emotion, like a spray can in a fire. I can open, and as I learn to open, I can allow myself to love and to be loved.

NATURE

As I came home through the woods with my string of fish,
trailing my pole, it being now quite dark, I caught a glimpse
of a woodchuck stealing across my path, and felt a strange
thrill of savage delight, and was strongly tempted to seize
and devour him raw; not that I was hungry then, except for
that wildness which he represented. Once or twice, however,
while I lived at the pond, I found myself ranging the woods,
like a half-starved hound, with a strange abandonment, seeking
some kind of venison which I might devour, and no morsel
could have been too savage for me. The wildest scenes had become
unaccountably familiar. I found in myself, and still find, an
instinct toward the higher, or, as it is named, spiritual life, as do
most men, and another toward a primitive rank and savage
one, and I reverence them both.

—HENRY DAVID THOREAU,
Walden

NATURE REVEALS OUR NATURE. OUR INNER NATURE OR
essence or soul is what we are born with; it is who we really
are by heredity and temperament—my essential "Tracy"—
as opposed to all the ideas and attitudes that have been
grafted on to our personality in the course of our education
and upbringing.[1] Essence is archetypal emotion, from exquisite to base, Thoreau's "spiritual" and "savage" alike.

Essence is deeply buried in most of us, but over time the

forces of nature, which are manifest in the great ordeals of life, can uncover it. Great feelings like grief and love and sex show us what is finest and what is rawest in our inner nature, just as great physical challenges and illnesses do. More subtle experiences of nature—the sound of the ocean, the sight of a particular face, a soft touch—can awaken essence as well. Essence is pure emotion, but it is close to the body. It is the part of us that values what it means to be alive on the earth. As we awaken to essence and welcome it into our conscious life, it suffuses us with an energy that makes us feel—not just think—that we are part of the oneness of life.

The kinship between the forces of nature and our essence is dramatically apparent in the ceremonies and beliefs of the nature religion of Santeria. One autumn day several years after I was mugged, Margot Torres, a diminutive, elderly Cuban woman, picked me up in a penny-colored Cadillac in front of a café near our apartment on East 6th Street and Avenue A and took me to a Santeria ceremony on the Upper West Side. Margot, who is a much respected *madrina,* or guide, had explained to me that Santeria is a nature religion that traces its roots back two thousand years to the height of the civilization of the West African kingdom of the Yoruba. The Yoruba brought their religion to the New World as slaves. *Santeros*—practitioners of Santeria—who fled Castro's Cuba, Margot among them, brought the religion to New York City in 1959.

"We hear the voices of the ancestors, the spirits of the ancient slaves," said Margot in the car that day. "We are never alone." The young Cuban man who drove nodded.

In the weeks before, while researching an article on Santeria for *New York Magazine,* I had discovered that this secretive religion of the ancient slaves was becoming a cultural force in the city, catching the hearts and imaginations of white artists and intellectuals. Still, the vast majority of the millions who practice Santeria in this country are people of color from Third World countries. Of the almost five hundred people who visited the ceremony I attended, I was the only white American.

In the car, Margot gave me white beads to wear for protection and rubbed ocher powder into my face to shield me from the evil eye. "There may be people who aren't so good there," she said. She gripped my arm when we arrived at the ceremony, held in the basement of a high-rise apartment building on West 93rd Street. The host, a big, expansive man, welcomed me graciously but others eyed me with mistrust. Several of the *santeros* I had interviewed had warned me that there is a lingering prejudice in Santeria against white Americans because *santeros* see them as representing the worldview that had made slaves of the Yoruba and forced them to pretend that they were worshipping Catholic saints. Margot told people in Spanish that I had a special right to be at the ceremony because I was a twin and because this was a ceremony for Shango, the *orisa,* or god, who loves and protects twins.

In a big back room, the two-headed *bata* drums made the air pulsate with intricate rhythms that were meant to salute the *orisas.* A crowd standing four deep around the room clapped and chanted; at intervals, when a new *orisa* was welcomed, we bowed. A group split off and began to dance. The room grew hotter and the vibrations from the relentless drumming were so palpable that it seemed as if we were all being pulled into a magnetic force field. The dancers gave themselves up to the drumming, serene and absorbed, as tiny Margot stood by me and followed the increasingly complex and driven rhythms with the erect bearing of an African queen.

In Santeria, water, wind, fire, trees—every element in nature—are seen as homes for one or another of the *orisas,* who are archetypal forces or personas. The *orisa* Shango manifests in fire, thunder, and displays of strength, while the female *orisa* Oya manifests her force in tornadoes and strong winds, in fire, lightning, and buffalo. Humans who have accomplished great deeds can also be immortalized as *orisas,* and, as Margot explained, the spirits of ancient slaves are also part of the firmament as an honored subclass called *preto velho.*

After saluting all the *orisas,* the drums focused on calling Shango down into the bodies of the dancers. A dancer, our host, lurched like a drunk and stopped. His head sagged on his chest, his body convulsed; he began to dance again and staggered. When he lifted his head, he was completely changed from the genial man who had greeted me. His eyes, which had been crinkled up in ebullient hospitality, were now wide and staring; his upper lip stretched down in a cunning, nakedly competitive look. Earlier he had rushed about like a restaurant owner on a busy night; now he strutted. All his gestures grew huge and imperious. He kicked off his shoes and bleated to the crowd, demanding that people come forward and serve him. Shango, the fiery, powerful king, had seated himself in our host's head.

Santeros believe that when we are born the head of each of us contains a drop of a sacred substance that belongs to a particular *orisa,* an *orisa* we have chosen before birth. Our chosen *orisa* is literally "owner of the head," and when people formally give themselves to their *orisa* in an initiation, that *orisa* is crowned or enthroned or seated in the head. After the initiation, the *orisa* becomes a powerful guardian angel, a wish-granting higher force. But the *orisas* are not to be toyed with and discarded. "I see initiation in terms of learning to serve a very powerful and potentially disintegrating force," one white American *santera* told me. "It can't abandon you and you don't dare break the contract with it. It can blow you apart."

Another *santero,* a master drummer, explained to me that the *orisas* mete out rewards and punishments according to a kind of instant karma. "The *orisas* will give you plenty of warnings if you're doing something wrong," he said. "But if you don't shape up they will punish you, and whatever may hurt you the most may be your punishment."

At the ceremony on West 93rd Street, mighty Shango was being honored for all the help he had given our host. Dressed in a red satin tunic and a crown, he was led to an altar ringed with offerings of food and money. Shango blessed people who prostrated before him, and he advised and chastised and embraced them. *Santeros* hung on his every word. Joy, and sometimes fear or flickers of shame, washed over their faces because they believed they were communing with a great elemental force, a sacred being who could bring clarity and order to their lives.

Margot, indifferent to whispered protests and cold glances, pulled me through the crowd toward Shango. I was a twin, she admonished them again. Gently, Shango demonstrated how to cross my arms in front of my chest to receive a blessing. He brushed me down the front and down the back with the broad side of his ritual double-headed axe. Margot's eyes shone as she watched.

"Well, you've been saved," said the young Cuban man who drove us to the ceremony. "From what, I don't know." Around us swirled five more dancers possessed by Shango. I felt the balm of devotion spread through the room like a slow wave.

Days later, back in the East Village, I thought about the world that Margot and the other *santeros* lived in. "There is an energy, an *ashe,* which moves the world," Margot had explained. "We can't see it, but it exists." *Ashe,* I had learned, is a cosmic energy that is saturated with the divine force or lifeblood of God. *Santeros* believe that God, whom many of them know by the Yoruba name of *Olodumare,* is incarnated constantly and everywhere as *ashe.* They believe that this God force is channeled to us through our connection to our ancestors, and that it is brought down to us in the rainbow of energies represented by the *orisas.*

I admired the wildness, the emotional power, of the *orisas.* Like Greek gods, they experienced human passions on a grand scale; they were neither unequivocally good nor bad, creative nor destructive, but representations of human feelings and attributes in their essential form. Since my mugging, I had become intrigued by the amorality of the passions and events that can be transforming in the spiritual life. I found myself cherishing an act of violence against myself—the mugging—as a means toward something sacred. I had even dreamed that I was being mugged by Jesus. "Do you think I'm hurting you?" he asked, as he opened me to the light. In my dream, Jesus was a beautiful homeless outsider who waited in the shadows for people who were vulnerable to transformation. His impact on people was too great and too dangerous for him ever to be considered socially acceptable or good. Later, I came across this passage from Oscar Wilde's letter from prison, *De Profundis:*

The world had always loved the saint as being the nearest possible approach to the perfection of God. Christ, through some divine instinct in him, seems to have always loved the sinner as being the nearest possible approach to the perfection of man. His primary desire was not to reform people any more than his desire was to relieve suffering.... But in a manner not yet understood of the world, he regarded sin and suffering as being in themselves beautiful holy things and modes of perfection.

I had found that transformation can take place even in a dark circumstance. I also knew that the light that had seemed to pierce my chest with such grave love had been searching for something deeper than thought—something too deep to be defined by moral judgments about good or bad. The "me" that the light had finally seemed to locate was wordless and mysterious, utterly apart from all the heady struggles and opinions that tell me who I am. It was connected to some primal sense and feeling for my existence. I knew that I would never grow spiritually, never find a way to transform, unless I found this unknown part of me. I knew that it was separate from my mind, and that it had been so buried under the layers of my personality that it was like a wild child, unable to communicate directly and easily spooked. Yet I knew that the exquisite feeling I'd had in the presence of the light—the wish to serve the higher—had been that same child. It had *felt* the sacred and responded with innate grace.

I knew nothing about the inner alchemy of the possession trance, but I had seen that the *santeros* who had been chosen by Shango were not acting. They were pouring real emotion, real passion into an archetypal form, a general emotional type, that had been made present by the rhythm of the drums. They all acted alike, adopting huge exaggerated gestures that were both regal and earthy. They had swaggered and roared the way ancient kings would, indifferent to what others thought.

To this outsider, the *santeros* who were possessed seemed to be hypnotized, their personalities put to sleep, so that a deeper, purer strata of feeling could be exposed. Shango's energy, his psychic archetype, was conjured up by the drums, and it seemed to target particular types of *santeros*. Shango's "types"—the types who had been prepared through initiation to receive this energy—were invited to come out and dance and strut and shout and experience their untamed, inherent divinity.

I was aware that I would never know what it feels like to be possessed by an *orisa*. To me, the *orisas* were reminders that while essence is emotional, it is also physical, allowing it to be touched by ancient rhythms and archetypal postures. Santeria taught me that the natural world is full of an energy that can infuse us with a sense of the true magic of reality, if only we knew how to drink it in.

"These energies are around us all the time," said the master drummer I spoke to. "The drums just tap into them."

> *For I have learned*
> *To look on nature, not as in the hour*
> *Of thoughtless youth; but hearing oftentimes*
> *The still, sad music of humanity,*
> *Nor harsh nor grating, though of ample power*
> *To chasten and subdue. And I have felt*
> *A presence that disturbs me with the joy*
> *Of elevated thoughts; a sense sublime*
> *Of something far more deeply interfused,*
> *Whose dwelling is the light of setting suns,*
> *And the round ocean and the living air,*
> *And the blue sky, and in the mind of man:*
> *A motion and a spirit, that impels*
> *All thinking things, all objects of thought,*
> *And rolls through all things.*
>
> —WILLIAM WORDSWORTH,
> from *Lines Composed a Few Miles*
> *Above Tintern Abbey*

As I walked through the East Village, thinking about the magical connections I saw at the Santeria ceremony, I came upon a scene that showed me something about how essence can be turned toward the sacred, toward the spirit that Wordsworth said "rolls through all things," even in this gritty urban neighborhood that I had always thought of as life after nature.

A tribe of adolescents stood in front of a graffiti-covered bar called Alcatraz, trading drags off cigarettes and drinking coffee and swigging beer out of green bottles. Their hair was dyed magenta and the blue-black of ravens' wings, or their heads were shaved. Ears, eyebrows, and noses were pierced, and most arms were tattooed. Boys and girls alike wore black, lug-soled boots and black leather jackets. What struck me, though, was the tenderness and vulnerability in their eyes. These kids slouched about with mock indifference, their faces impassive, but their eyes were wide open and tender—these were eyes that noticed things.

Watching these young men and women, I could see the impulse in them to hide away what they really felt. It seemed to me that they wanted to know the meaning of their existence and they didn't want to know it just with their heads: They wanted to feel it in their hearts. I could see that there was something buried in them, something that wished to be. At certain moments in our lives, we can feel this something pushing forward, searching for a corresponding energy.

The restlessness and yearning of these young men and women were written in their eyes. They had come together because they wanted to embark on a journey they couldn't name. Something in them wanted to move. They wanted to experience something different, to find an identity that was bigger than anything they could find in isolation. Sometimes, I knew, you could be more yourself in a group. You could drop the prison of your fear and emerge as a human being among other humans. And here was the answer to my question: Even in the city, I realized, we can sense the power of nature—and the presence of that wellspring of meaning that we call the sacred—in one another. I remembered something that Margot Torres had once told me. "I live in a world," she had said. "But everyone is part of this world." In this world, we bring the sacred to each other.

Ah, what can ever be more stately and admirable to me than
  mast-hemm'd Manhattan?
River and sunset and scallop-edg'd waves of flood-tide?
The sea-gulls oscillating their bodies, the hay-boat in
the twilight, and the
  belated lighter?
What gods can exceed these that clasp me by the hand,
and with voices I
  love call me promptly and loudly by my nighest
name as I approach?
What is more subtle than this which ties me to the
woman or man that looks
  in my face?
Which fuses me into you now, and pours meaning into you?
  —WALT WHITMAN,
  from *Crossing Brooklyn Ferry*

A. R. Orage, England's most respected and influential literary editor in the early years of this century, had this to say about essence:

Essence is truth about oneself in contrast to social and expected opinions of oneself. Essence is truth irrespective of time, place, and the feelings of anyone. It is what one would dare to avow if no consequences were to follow on a statement of the truth. It is truth before God. Personality is truth before men—before the world, conditioned by "What will people think?"

It is necessary to know what you really wish. As you discover your real wish, external circumstances will change and
become more like those you wish.[2]

One day while walking in the Brooklyn Botanical Gardens, I tried to find my "truth before God." Focusing on the
beauty around me, I let go of all thoughts of other people
and patiently waited for my essence to send up a sign. I was
surprised when a real wish, a question that did not come
from my head, *did* appear. At first it stung like a wound exposed to the air, but it filled me with energy and a sense of
emerging back into the world. I find this exercise useful to
try when I need direction.

CREATIVITY

Everything *is gestation and then birthing. To let each impression and each embryo of a feeling come to completion, entirely in itself, in the dark, in the unsayable, the unconscious, beyond the reach of one's own understanding, and with deep humility and patience to wait for the hour when a new clarity is born: this alone is what it means to live as an artist: in understanding as in creating.*[1]

—RAINER MARIA RILKE

ONE FALL DAY IN 1994, WHILE JEFF TOOK ALEXANDRA TO play in a park, I stood at the bottom of a scaffold outside the west front of the Cathedral of St. John the Divine in Manhattan, watching master sculptor Simon Verity chip away at a slab of Indiana limestone that was gradually becoming an eight-foot-tall statue of John the Baptist. Verity, a slight, handsome Englishman with wild brown hair threaded with grey, stood with his back to me in the wind, and I had to call up to him twice before he turned.

With the help of a young French stonecutter and various apprentices, for the past five years, from spring until fall, Verity has spent eight to ten hours a day up on the scaffold, slowly and intuitively carving a procession of thirty-two patriarchs and matriarchs that lead churchgoers through

"The Portal of Paradise" on just one day a year, Easter. The portal, with its vast, bronze "Easter doors," symbolizes the entrance to Christ's tomb, and the people who flow inside are meant to feel transformed. John the Baptist, Abraham, Sarah, and all the other figures Verity has carved stand watch above, looking mysterious, impersonal, like representatives from another world.

"I'm looking for something other when I carve them," Verity explained. "They're not connected to this world. They're in another place, in their heavenly robes."

We had settled on a bench in the biblical garden in back of the cathedral, holding steaming cups of coffee from the Hungarian Pastry Shop across the street. I was meeting Verity to talk about transforming moments in creative work.

"I've had moments of real connection with my work," Verity told me. "I feel as if a spark has leapt and then it's gone. These moments aren't continuous. I keep trying to get more of a flow, to allow more without trying to control so much."

"How can we extend these moments of connection?" he asks. "That's the question and that's what's so painful. You have the sense of this opening, this other energy passing through, and it's utter bliss when it happens—but it's transitory. I think this is what any artist is searching for. What drives you on is that you know that it's there and it's just a question of getting out of the way."

St. John the Divine is a sacred space, according to Verity. The geometry of its proportions is designed to fill us with a sense of the presence of God, just as in the great medieval cathedrals. The stone carver sees the doorway that he has been laboring over as a kind of funnel, drawing people inside into a sacred space and sending them back out in the world, infused with the finer energies—the impressions of the sacred—that are circulating within.

"In the thirteenth century people used geometry to describe God and the cosmos," Verity told me. "They understood that we're all connected and that all life is connected. When they came together to build these extraordinary structures, there was a sense of everybody coming together for a common purpose. People were building blocks in a greater whole and individual egos weren't so important. What I'm trying is part of this medieval tradition—working with the sense that we're all connected in a unified whole."

Verity and I talked about how meditation can pull us out of our thoughts and restore us to the sense of being present in the world—which, we agreed, is probably a first step towards sensing our connection to the whole. He said his work was sometimes like meditation.

"There's something in the repetitive action of the work," he explained. "I'm hitting that stone once every second for two hours, and then I stop work for twenty minutes, and then I begin again, and for eight or ten hours a day, that's what I do. That's extraordinary, isn't it? And I've been doing that for thirty years. And that's a very strange thing to be doing."

I walked away from Verity thinking that it really is a strange and wonderful thing that he does. I crossed the street from the cathedral, threading my way through traffic, passing a clutch of Columbia University students dressed in big baggy sweaters and black leather jackets, and a furious homeless man who lurched down the middle of Amsterdam Avenue, screaming about conspiracy and shaking his fist at cars that bothered to honk. I turned back and saw Verity up on the scaffold, above the urban chaos, trying to be mindful, trying not to be distracted as he chipped away at two square inches of limestone. Watching his hammer strike his chisel once a second, it occurred to me that Simon Verity is living at the heart of the creative process.

> When and how [my ideas] come I know not; nor can I force them ... provided that I am not disturbed, my subject enlarges itself and becomes methodized and defined and the whole, though it be long, stands almost complete and finished in my mind, so that I can survey it, like a fine picture or a beautiful statue—at a glance nor do I hear in my imagination the parts successively, but I hear them, as it were, all at once. What a delight this is, I cannot tell. All this inventing, this producing takes place in a pleasing lively dream.[2]
> —WOLFGANG AMADEUS MOZART

Few of us have had a creative experience comparable to the one Mozart describes, yet many of us, in the midst of creative work, have experienced moments of illumination or inspiration in which the painting seems to be painting itself, or the solution to the science or business problem we've been struggling with flashes into our mind while we're taking a walk or digging in the garden. These moments often feel like openings or clearings. Without warning, we emerge from the dense cover of our habitual thoughts and doings, encountering the material of our work in a fresh, direct way. Our work feels effortless and we may feel buoyed up by an energy that shows why "inspiration" literally means "infused with spirit" or with the "breath" of the divine. We may feel in sync with the world around us, not hunched over our work table struggling in isolation—though long, hard stretches of labor may have preceded this moment—but receiving impressions and ideas from a higher or a deeper part of ourselves that is suddenly able to come through.

These moments of creative insight or intuition are very close to experiences of awakening because they show us that what we usually identify as the self is just a fraction of who we really are. These moments reveal that there is a submerged part in us that is attuned to reality with mysterious subtlety and intelligence. When it sends us a valentine—a solution or a vision—it reminds us that we are an unknown waiting to be explored and that we are connected to the world in ways we do not understand.

The tiniest flashes of insight seem miraculous to me because I am familiar with the pain of trying to make something happen. A dozen years ago, I took a painting class. I was so determined to be a good painter right away that I lost all sense of painting as a process. I fell into a kind of compulsive perfectionism that had Jeff looking on in worried fascination. One evening, I stood before an easel in our East Village living room and painted and repainted one eye in a self-portrait for hours until the eye went from dead accurate to grotesquely overdone. It was the visual equivalent of perfectionism with words, where a writer gets trapped in a loop of words that have lost all connection to reality. Slowly, I learned that letting go can take me farther than my mental efforts ever could. As William James described in *The Varieties of Religious Experience*:

> You know how it is when you try to recollect a forgotten name. Usually you help the recall by working for it, by mentally running over the places, persons, and things with which the word was connected. But sometimes this effort fails: you feel then as if the harder you tried the less hope there would be, as though the name were *jammed,* and pressure in its direction only kept it all the more from rising. And then the opposite expedient often succeeds. Give up the effort en-

tirely; think of something altogether different, and in half an hour the lost name comes sauntering into your mind, as Emerson says, as carelessly as if it had never been invited. Some hidden process was started in you by the effort, which went on after the effort ceased, and made the result come as if it came spontaneously.[3]

I learned that creative intuition depends on an unconscious process of gestation, a ripening that cannot be forced or faked. In the past century, Western psychology has attempted to isolate the stages of the creative process. In the most widely accepted analysis, developed by psychologist Graham Wallas, the process is broken down into four stages. An initial preparation period—a period of conscious study, struggle, and play—gives way to an incubation period in which the unconscious orders and reorders and generally mulls over the material. This gestation gives birth to a moment of illumination or intuition in which the creator experiences mind and perception blazing open to reveal a new pattern or even a new reality; finally, in cases of scientific work, the work is examined for accuracy. This paradigm of a flash of intuition following long labor accounts, for example, for how Einstein was able to conceive of his general and special theories of relativity.

In his book *The Mind of God: The Scientific Basis for a Rational World,* the physicist Paul Davies describes how some scientists and mathematicians have had sudden illuminations that are very close to mystical awakenings. He mentions how mathematician Kurt Gödel reportedly "spoke of the 'other relation to reality,'" a relation that Gödel apparently cultivated through "meditative practices."[4] Davies also offers this account of a revelation that came to cosmologist and science fiction author Fred Hoyle as he was driving through the North of England:

> As the miles slipped by I turned the quantum mechanical problem … over in my mind, in the hazy way I normally have in thinking mathematics in my head. Normally, I have to write things down on paper, and then fiddle with the equations and integrals as best I can. But somewhere on Bowes Moor my awareness of the mathematics clarified, not a little, not even a lot, but as if a huge brilliant light had suddenly been switched on. How long did it take to become totally convinced that the problem was solved? Less than five seconds.[5]

There is no formula for such a breakthrough, but there are common elements in all scientific and artistic work that lead to breakthroughs. Above all, there is the necessity of much hard work, of slow, incremental increases in skill, craft, and knowledge. Many great artists have insisted on the value of effort and work over inspiration; genius, as it's said, is 99 percent perspiration and 1 percent inspiration. Yet the value of hard work lies not just in the sheer labor (which probably does cultivate us in all kinds of seen and unseen ways) but in training the attention.

All acts of creativity are rooted in attention—not just the ordinary attention of the mind but a sensitive, all-embracing attentiveness that includes body, feeling, and mind: the same attentiveness that is essential to spiritual work. Perhaps this is why many traditional spiritual paths include the teaching of a creative discipline. Tibetan monks are known for their intricate sand paintings and *thangka*s; Zen monks, for their brushwork and haiku; Christian monks, for their illuminated manuscripts and wines.

In order to work, in order to be excited, in order to simply be, you have to be reborn to the instant. You have to permit yourself to feel ... to be vulnerable. You may not like what you see, that is not important. But you must be attacked by it, excited by it, and your body must be alive.[6]

—MARTHA GRAHAM

We can't predict when or where a moment of illumination will emerge from the unconscious depths, but our chances of being struck by lightning are better when we are out in the open. It is in the present that creative work converges with the spiritual because it is only in the present moment that we can be aware of the forces of life entering us, sinking into that buried part of ourselves that Rilke said is "beyond the reach of one's own understanding." And it is only by making ourselves vulnerable to the present—which is a wild place, an unknown—that we can begin to be sensitive to the movements in the deepest reaches of ourselves and to be truly open to those moments of authentic response. Such a moment of creative response or intuition can be transforming because it can show us that what we may really be is a channel or a conduit for the transmission of forces that come down from above and meet those that rise up from the ground of our being. To be present to the way we work, we must, it seems, become a bit like the sacred space of the cathedral as Simon Verity described it. We have to let go of any rigid sense of what we are and what we want and become a sensitive responsiveness; then we may discover that we are sacred in this world not for any possessions or fixed traits, but because of our emptiness—because of what we might hold.

The creator, like a spiritual seeker, needs to be led not by certainty but by questioning—a questioning that is so intense that it is also an engagement, an entering in. Watching children, who are natural artists and explorers, it's easy to see that, fundamentally, human beings create to create and explore to explore—for the sheer joy of it. What they produce, what they find, is of secondary concern. "I remember loving fossils when I was a boy," Simon Verity told me. "I've always been astonished by the beauty of them." Einstein explained that he was able to come up with his theories of relativity because he allowed himself to think about subjects—space and time—that ordinarily only children think about. This fresh, direct way of seeing is what Zen Buddhists call "beginner's mind."

To be a true artist or scientist it is necessary to be a risk taker who can leave the known behind. Picasso thought of his canvases as "researches" and insisted that all of them were different ways of posing the same question. Real artists, wrote the painter Wassily Kandinsky in 1914 in *The Art of Spiritual Harmony,* seek "the 'inner' by way of the 'outer'.... Cézanne [for example] ... was endowed with the gift of divining the inner life in everything."

"So-called creators sometimes do have an opening to another reality that's behind this reality," said William Segal, a painter and writer in his 90s who walks with the precision of a Zen abbot. Segal has bright kind eyes and a Brooklyn accent burnished by years spent in New York, Paris, and Japan. "But there are many manifestations of the unlocking or opening of a reality of deeper perception."

I was talking with Segal in his apartment on the Upper East Side of Manhattan. He wore a black eyepatch over one eye, and in the midst of talking to me he gently excused himself to go and get a big green parrot that perched on his shoulder during the rest of our time together, adding to the rakish elegance that somehow underlined the soft-spoken certainty of his words. Segal isn't well known to the general public, yet many interested in Buddhism and other spiritual traditions regard him as a man of real spiritual attainment. He has never allowed himself to be labeled as an expert on, or spokesperson for, a particular tradition, and this simple authenticity, this dedication to the truth of lived experience rather than abstractions, inhabits everything he says.

"Some people have a feeling of inquiry," Segal told me. "They want to know more, and they learn through painting or through music or through expressing themselves. But very often an accident, or a moment of great sorrow or shock, brings insights that we don't ordinarily have."

One possible explanation for these "openings," or sudden perceptions of another reality, according to Segal, is that some of the energies that run through our bodies obscure finer and more subtle energies. We're too often blinded, in other words, by our preoccupations with food or sex or getting and spending.

"If I'm totally engaged in eating, for example," Segal said, "my thinking and my feeling, my sensitivities, might be a little bit nonoperative at that moment. If one could be pure in the sense that the currents of energy are running as they should—not colliding with each other or obscuring each other—the organs of perception would be operating in quite a different way. We would see things differently, hear things differently.

"We can only see what our eyes see, we can only hear what our ears hear, we can only taste what our taste buds convey to us," he added, "but another entity's eyesight, their hearing, their tasting apparatus, their organs of perception bring them data quite differently. The senses are messengers that convey material from nature; as I look at you I see an image but I only see this image according to my perceptive capacities. This parrot on my shoulder might see you quite differently—it might see you as a ball of light. Now, when our configuration is a little different, at that moment we might have quite a different perception. This would bring the illumination that we're speaking of. These are the moments or experiences of insight or intuition that inspired artists, composers, and poets speak of."

I asked Segal how we could go about changing the configuration of our perceptions to experience insight. I described how I had felt my ordinary faculties surrendering their usual grip when I was mugged.

"A rearrangement of the perceptual apparatus probably is a necessary element in experiencing or perceiving things differently," he said. "In silence one has a different feeling and a different relation with the world outside and inside. It is possible to develop or cultivate [opening] if you wish, to develop being more open and sensitive to the world we live in."

This moment-by-moment effort to be present and still makes infinitely more sense than imagining that we can escape the hold of our usual way of seeing things in one definitive act of surrender, according to Segal.

"But we don't let go, we don't surrender," he told me, "so very often it's only in moments of shock or intense suffering that this opening takes place. Ordinarily, we're asleep and we go along with the mechanical flow of things, and we can't experience very much outside of the ordinary experiencings that we're bound to have. Nature is always pulling at us, making us a little tense or a little sleepy. Our organism is geared to perform a certain function in life. We have to eat and transform food, we have to sleep, we have to have sex, we have to be engaged in all these activities. We're so busy fulfilling the demands of nature, as we should be, that we rarely have time to bring about this stop, which is a prelude to opening."

Segal brushed aside questions about his own painting career with a wave of his hand.

"The human organism is capable of all kinds of receptivities. We know from quantum physics that the objects we see are illusory. The world is full of invisible realities, but if people do not see or hear them these realities do not exist."

After a while, Segal ushered me into a little study where we watched a short videotape that the documentary filmmaker Ken Burns had made to introduce an exhibition of Segal's work in Japan.

"I think in painting one is brought to see in a different way," says Segal in the videotape. "Ordinarily we're rather asleep to the world around us, and being forced to look and then to render in paint or on paper compels one to look both inward and outward, to learn a little bit more about the nature of oneself as well as learning about the nature of things." The camera takes in the paintings that fill Segal's rambling house in New Jersey. The simple still lifes and self-portraits match Kandinsky's description of the works of Cézanne; they emanate an inner life, expressed through a quality that Segal calls "luminosity."

"In a way the artist is a revealer, a revealer of a world that is ordinarily hidden from us," he adds. "Luminosity is a mysterious element which is a reflection of a higher world which sometimes enters your world and my world through a face, through an apple, through a painting. It's always here, this luminosity, but it's so densely hidden. Luminosity is always around us all the time, in everything, but the painter who has a certain quality in himself is able to evoke this on a canvas."

Segal vivifies this quality through a story.

"I had a studio on 14th Street in New York and I would work over the weekend, and I was a hard worker. I had been painting for two or three or four hours, just painting and then suddenly [it was] as if the brush was painting by itself. And I stepped back in surprise ... and there was a beautiful piece of painting within a bad large painting. And I suddenly said to myself, 'My God, there's something here that goes beyond applying paint on a canvas,' and it indicated to me that through continuing to paint, persisting, there will come a moment when there is an opening which will teach you what I cannot speak about or tell you. [It is] as if you suddenly know something. It may not be much, but it's something that you didn't know before. And at that moment I said, 'Well, I have to keep going. Maybe I'm not so talented but if I keep looking and looking, trying to be here....' One [can have] a breakthrough moment.

"The great energy is here, and our responsibility is to open to it," adds Segal in Ken Burns's videotape, and the warm brown eye that is not covered by the patch shines with joy at the adventure of it all. "Through painting, the painter is able to let this other force come through."

Burns's camera lingers on Segal at twilight, sitting on the edge of his porch in the country. He is wearing linen trousers, a linen waistcoat, and a big straw hat, like a French painter from another century, and he is carefully lighting a Japanese lantern.

"Forget everything except what is here, now, in front of you, because only by ... being here are you able to tap the full resources of the organism. Otherwise the distraction of thought eats up energies which could be used and applied to the work itself.

"The demand to be here, to maintain attention for a sustained period of time, kind of dispels the clouds which obscure the luminosity we're speaking of. . . . I'd like to see a wholehearted application to the moment . . . that's very much the secret of good work in anything."

After we watched the film, Segal and I talked a bit longer. Just before I stood to leave, I blurted out to him that I had experienced small moments of a broader awareness when I allowed myself to be present and attentive to what I was doing, but that I had never since seen or felt the hidden luminous world as I had that night in Hell's Kitchen.

"You can't be greedy for an experience that was given to you," said Segal. "But even in very ordinary relationships there are possibilities that we're not utilizing." He picked up a piece of writing paper. "When you pick up a piece of paper . . . you look at it all day long but if you really saw it, what a wonderful thing it could be. Or when you write, the movements of the hand.

"These accumulations of moments of awakening begin to show you another world, so just be patient," he advised. "You know the way. It's a question of practicing. There's a great biblical saying that goes in this direction: 'Be still, and know that I am.'"

An experiment that I have tried several times is to pick a small activity to perform with all of my attention, each day for a week. If this interests you, I suggest you spend ten to thirty minutes each day doing the activity, staying present and quietly attentive to this simple task. Don't worry if your mind wanders; just notice the wandering and then bring your attention back to the activity at hand. For example, you might choose to draw your face as it is reflected in a mirror. Or you might handwrite a letter or a journal entry describing something exactly as it really looks, smells, tastes, or feels—what's important is that the activity involve quiet work with your hands. Another possibility is to prepare breakfast carefully. Even if it's just toast and coffee, put great care into the fixing and presentation, as if you were preparing it for a loved one. Try to make the preparation take at least ten minutes, and then try to devote an equal amount of time and care to eating the meal. On the last day, spend at least ten minutes sitting and quietly reflecting on your impressions of the previous six days.

Cyberspace

Suddenly I don't have a body anymore.[1]
—John Perry Barlow,
cofounder of the Electronic Frontier
Foundation,on first entering virtual reality

It's shortly after 9:00 in the evening on a cold December night and I'm deep in conversation with a woman who calls herself "nina." She's telling me about how, while photographing her spiritual teacher giving a talk, she experienced a moment of mystical unity. I don't know nina's real name, if she's twenty-five or sixty-five, tall, short, thin, fat, pretty or plain, the color of her hair or eyes, if her voice is coarse or smooth, or what she does for a living. Still, our talk is lively and meaningful, and I find myself opening up to her in unexpected ways.

Nina and I aren't talking in person or over the telephone. We're communicating online, each typing words onto a computer keyboard, with our respective computers linked via modem to ECHO, or East Coast Hang Out, a Manhattan-based "virtual community" of about 3,500 citizens. On ECHO, people generally talk with one another by "posting" sequential messages in public "conferences" where they identify themselves, as is customary throughout the online world, by handles, or pseudonyms; my handle is "Prodigal

Sun aka Jeff Zaleski." The conference nina and I are logged onto is called "Into the Mystic." As we post messages that will be seen by others but that are directed to one another, our conversation scrolls onto my computer screen like this:

130:6)nina   27-DEC-94 21:15

One of the most precious experiences of my life was two years ago. I have had a teacher for the past ten years, and two summers ago I had the good fortune to photographically document a particularly large event in her attendance. I had been awake for about seventy-two hours and my tripod was holding me up. Although I was very into being there, it seemed like everything was taking soooo long. At last, it was time for her to speak ... and I started to experience the most excruciating pains in my head. I thought I was going to pass out and I was really mad, as this was what I really wanted to be shooting. I looked down the barrel of my lens to see her looking right back—a *very* unusual occurrence. She was in the middle of a sentence and she stopped, not moving her eyes. She said, "Some people have headaches ... so much to get rid of," and then returned to the sentence she had not completed before, readdressing the crowd. My mind went into complete and total time warp. There, hanging in the midst of all time happening at once, I stood, saturated with a moment of clarity. There was no sound, no feeling, no pressure—yet a totally full void. I knew everything in that second—and damn if I didn't forget it twenty minutes later when I didn't find the roll of film I was looking for. The point is, at that moment, I knew how she knew, even though I was fifty feet away from her in a crowd of three thousand. And I was her, and the crowd, and me/she/they were simply that. No difference, no separation, simple, sweet ecstasy.

Infinite compassion, and knowledge. I have been hungrier than ever to attain that permanently.

130:7)Prodigal Sun aka Jeff Zaleski   27-DEC-94 21:34

Great post, thanks. This moment of absolute clarity—it's so extraordinary and yet seems so . . . right, even normal, when it comes. At least that's my experience. I'm guessing that your "teacher" is some sort of spiritual friend or guide to you. I've also had moments when a sudden gaze or word from a teacher crashed through my dreaming and brought me back to reality. I guess that's one reason we need them. Your comment about hungering to have the experience again strikes home with me, too; it's something I've thought about. Because I've been told more than once that this kind of hunger, instead of just accepting what is in the present moment, can get in the way of spiritual work. But I don't know . . . these touchstones are such delicious carrots, and I'm such a lazy donkey—I need to be inspired.

130:8)nina   27-DEC-94 21:41

Yes—how can you get somewhere if you don't know where you are going and you don't have a map? Yes, I mean spiritual teacher. And, yes, the irony of these rare moments is that they are what's really right and normal and they emphasize the absurdity of all the other nonrare moments. I think the greatest weapon for the spiritual warrior is an active sense of humor.

130:9)Prodigal Sun aka Jeff Zaleski   27-DEC-94 21:48

I couldn't agree with you more, and I think a sense of humor or lack of it tells a lot about a teacher, too. I think of the Dalai Lama, who's so free in laughing at his own

foibles—and him a god-king!—and two other renowned
spiritual teachers I've met, a Tibetan Dzogchen teacher and
a Turkish Sufi master, who wouldn't crack a smile if even
you tickled them with peacock feathers. They scared me …
but maybe that's a superficial response on my part?

130:10)nina   27-DEC-94 21:55

Nah … it's good to be scared of some teachers. I understand
that the stone face treatment is a lesson in itself. My teacher
laughs a great deal—yet, there have been moments when I
prayed that beloved face would stop looking so frozen. They
have to be fluid—I bet your Sufi master laughed himself silly
when he was by himself! …

I was talking to nina because Tracy and I wanted to explore moments of spiritual transformation not just through
the historical record but in the lives of contemporary men
and women. We wanted to learn what others considered to
be the transforming moments in their lives, and we hoped to
gather their stories of these moments. Going online seemed
an ideal way to do this. Not only would it allow us to reach
many people at once, but online communication, as I had
gathered from reading about it, can lead to a peculiar sort of
intimacy—an intimacy that we hoped would allow people
to reveal moments that they might not talk about on ques-
tionnaires. Since online communication takes place through
typing words onto a screen, moreover, it offers participants
time to reflect before responding, as well as the opportunity
to refine or correct their responses before posting, or sending, them—advantages not afforded in face-to-face or telephone interviews. On the other hand, I wondered whether

something would be lost by communicating with others only through a computer screen.

After buying a computer and modem, I joined the nation's three largest online services, America Online, CompuServe, and Prodigy, and posted a query inviting people to contribute their stories. I also posted a query on the Internet. Few people responded, however, in part because any particular query tends to get lost among the hundreds of others on these huge networks, but also, I realized later, because organizations like CompuServe, with its 2.7 million-plus subscribers, don't easily foster the sense of community, of shared experience, that permits people to reveal their secrets safely and comfortably. Of the responses I did receive, the most interesting was from William Turgeon, who teaches at the Waldorf School in Baltimore and who e-mailed me about a "visitation of peace" that came to him upon the death of his mother:

> My mother passed away in the spring of 1973, during my sophomore year in college, after fighting an inoperable cancer of the bronchial tubes. My younger sister and my four younger brothers, the youngest of which was nine, were still living at home. My mother had been receiving home care up until the week before her passing, and it remains with me today a strong impression and an expression of purpose and strength that she had "held on" long enough for me to see her upon my return home for the April break from school.
>
> Within a day or two after my arrival home, her condition worsened such that she had to be moved into the hospital. Late one evening in that early April, the hospital called our home to report that "her breathing had changed." This courteous representation of the hard truth of a loved one's passing is always and ever forgivable. At the hospital, by the

right-hand side of my mother's bedside, I fell into a heartfelt meditation of wonder and gratitude as I held with my own hands her wonderfully warm hand and arm. It was a most beautiful thought to know at that moment: This bodily warmth which I am touching and experiencing, though soon slowly to fade, is yet a real link to the individual person who has in these recent minutes vacated this physical abode.

I meditated in reverent gratitude upon that lingering sign and imprint of a departing human ego, if I may use that term.

Upon returning home with my father, brothers, and sister, we all gathered within the library of our home to hear the words my father wished to say. His simple message was: "Together we can go onward in the way that your mother would desire. We can do that if we love one another." I was sitting on the floor with my back against the wall, by the doorway to the room. During my father's "address" to the family, a most marvelous experience happened to me. As I listened to my father's words, a most profound peace and spiritual presence descended from above, coming downward upon me, encompassing me from the top of my head downward to my waist. This was not a subjectively inward experience but, to the contrary, was the objective sensation that this (unseen) "cloud of peace" was coming physically downward upon me from the direction above my head. It dwelt with me for possibly a minute to a minute and a half. In the way that it had descended, it slowly and calmly lifted vertically upward in the direction from which it had descended.

I was the only one in the room with this fortunate experience. My "cloud of peace" left no specific impression of whom or of what it may have been the signature. I have never really known the answer to that question, except that, for the first time, I am brought to wonder as I write these words whether it may not have been a reciprocated "thank you" mirroring in love the grateful meditation of the previous hour at my mother's bedside in the hospital.

Bill Turgeon's moving story made me eager to hear others. I was aware that scattered around the country were tens of thousands of smaller electronic services, some of them real virtual communities in that their members spoke with each other each day via modem, forming deep bonds of friendship, and sometimes of enmity. Happily, one online service located right in New York City and with a reputation for being smart and lively had been founded by my former wife, Stacy Horn. ECHO, which Stacy opened to the public in 1990, was also of interest because Tracy and I wanted to contact women as well as men, and few online services in the country approach ECHO's rate—38 percent —of female subscribers.

After getting Stacy's okay to post a query on ECHO, Tracy and I visited her in the West Village apartment where the service was then headquartered. In a room that was a pleasingly quirky blend of old and new, with dozens of gleaming modems and several laptop, desktop, and floor-standing computers competing for space with a huge antique armoire, Stacy set up our ECHO account and instructed us on how to connect to the service. That evening, I logged on to ECHO and connected to its eclectic membership, the majority of which lives in the New York area but which also draws from locations as far away as California, Rome, and even New Zealand. I posted my query and soon I was privy to some extraordinary stories. Here are three, each headlined by the handle of the person who posted it. All concern a transformative brush with death:

Posted by "Sne'ers-so-well <tm Danny>":

In the summer of 1986, I entered into a lucid dream one night. I was in a dark chamber, it felt like rock or something, with fog shifting about, and high, eerie, angelic voices singing in discord (listen to Lou Reed's "Berlin"—I can't remember the song at the moment, but those voices are there). And there was the stereotypical BRIGHT WHITE LIGHT, coming at medium intensity through the fog.

At that moment, I knew I was at what I call the Way Station. I felt very drawn toward the light. I knew if I went into it, I would die and enter another dimension. This knowledge made me very calm and happy. Yet I had a nagging sense it was not time—sort of like checking out dessert before you've eaten the main meal. It wasn't going anywhere and it just wasn't time yet.

So I exercised my will, forced myself awake to the point where I could speak. I was stuck in one of those states where you are mentally awake but physically paralyzed. I managed to wake my girlfriend, asking her to wake me up, because I was having "visions of death." She freaked and woke me up damn quick.

Since that night, I do not fear death.

Posted by "Knarf":

I remember when I was very young, probably around nine or ten, I had a dream that I'd fallen off a cliff and died. It was weird because it felt so real. I see myself floating away from the body. All my friends formed a circle around my body. I felt myself getting higher and higher until I was above the clouds. There was a short arched bridge made of brick. Just above it around the middle was sitting what I perceived as God and Jesus Christ. I walked across the bridge and stopped in the middle. I was being judged. As I looked at the other side of the bridge, I could make out all the people that I know that have died. Most prominent was my father. He was calling out to me. I wanted to run over to him, but somehow, I just couldn't. I heard a voice that said I wasn't ready yet and everything became a blur after that.

This dream made a big impact on how I looked at death from that point on. Death isn't painful. You won't miss anyone you leave behind. And you get to see the people you love that you have not seen in a long time.

Posted by "Magdalen":

About a year ago I was in a meditative state, somewhere between being awake and being asleep. I suddenly heard a voice talking about my heartbeat stopping, about my lungs stopping. Then I felt myself reeling forward into darkness. In the distance there was an even darker dark, a rectangular black hole of sorts. I knew suddenly that if I allowed myself to keep going, I wasn't going to come back. Another voice said to me, "Magdalen, it's not time yet. You have too much left to do. Go back, quickly, go back."

I forced myself to fight the current taking me forward and suddenly I was back in my body, except I couldn't breathe. My heart was pounding in my ears, but I couldn't get my breath. I forced myself up into a sitting position and suddenly started screaming, gasping for air.

It took me months to get over this enough to have a full night's sleep. My therapist said that sometimes the brain has a synapse or something like that and the spirit or whatever it is that we are starts to leave the body. It has had a profound impact on my life since then.

Curious about the "profound impact" of Magdalen's experience, I e-mailed her, asking her to elaborate. The reply she sent included these words:

The experience I had last year left me profoundly changed. The first week afterwards was intensely interior. I went on autopilot. I was going to work and coming home and laying on the couch in the fetal position. I felt like I was two people—one seemed like a shell, the outer me—the other felt like a stranger, distant, me, but not me. I couldn't sleep for that first week because I was afraid that I was going to die.

After a few weeks I started to come back to myself, realizing that the voice that told me to come back needed to be listened to, that I wasn't going to die so soon, at least not within the next few weeks. There was something I had to do.

A sense of urgency began to inform everything, bringing me closer to my son, yet informing my already impulsive nature and wreaking havoc in my marriage and at work. I didn't have any patience for anything ... I took the carpe diem philosophy too much to heart.

Things got worse before they got better. In April I got really sick. I started developing arthritic symptoms and others that led the doctors to think that I might have lupus or MS or some other awful, debilitating illness. I started to wonder if that episode back in the fall was a foreshadowing.

The positive result was that I was forced to really look at my symptoms and what they were telling me about my emotional/spiritual problems. I took my son up to Woodstock for the summer and spent several months reevaluating where I'm going.

There have been other episodes after that but more explainable. The fear from that experience informed anxiety attacks that left me debilitated for several days at a time.

It's only now, after a year, that I'm beginning to see how positive that experience was, that it had a lot to teach me. I was in a negative state of mind and being so all I focused on was the negative. I am beginning to realize that I was given an opportunity ... now I have to figure out what it really all meant. Any ideas?"

Not all the messages ECHO members posted or e-mailed were as dramatic as those just reproduced. Here, sent by a female ECHO subscriber who asks that she be referred to as "Delia"—neither her real name nor her handle—is an account of an unusual moment that emanates light and charm:

Last winter I took a writing class that focused on generating material rather than on technique. We worked with memories, favorite childhood stories, and images, and often did classroom exercises that combined relaxation and awareness techniques with rich sensory excursions into our imaginations, guided only by the slightest bit of structure from our instructor. (Visualization is the closest I can come to a description, but that seems too limited to one sense.)

At the time I felt unable to write and was really struggling with it, to little effect. During one of the exercises we imagined ourselves looking into a mirror where we saw a body of water and a person or being. I saw a rock jutting from the sea, and on it was a seal. Her face was beautiful and intelligent, but she seemed painfully clumsy and ungainly as she moved on the rock, and her fur was drying, sticking up in spikes. I wanted to do something to help but couldn't, and I felt very frustrated. She looked at me and told me it was all right. I still felt the urge to fix things, and again she said, "It's all right." I felt sad but sensed wisdom in what she said, so I just stayed with her until the water rose and she slipped into it and flashed away, graceful again.

This exercise didn't get me "material," but it made it easier to wait and be still until my writing was flowing again. And I've found that stillness at times of emotional turmoil, when I want to fix the way I feel or do something about it. I can tell myself "It's all right," and it gives me courage and patience to sit with whatever strong emotion I'm feeling.

As fascinating as these ECHO postings and messages were, as they grew in number I looked in vain for any that mentioned an awakening or transformation that had occurred to someone because they were online or while they were online—possibilities that I had asked about in my query. I wondered whether the silence indicated that something about cyberspace and the way we travel through it impedes our ability to awaken.

Each time I have explored unfamiliar territory, whether I was picking my way across the burial grounds of Pompeii, walking through a thicket of stalagmites in a cavern in the Black Hills of South Dakota, or circling in a helicopter above the skyscrapers of Manhattan, the novelty of the experience—the shock of the unexpected—has been strong enough to quiet my mind and allow my attention to expand to encompass the whole of myself, including my body. The first time I went online, sending an e-mail message to my brother Phil, this happened again; the uncanny sense of reaching out to someone through an electronically generated environment made me more aware of my body, not less. I had this same experience during my first foray into virtual reality, at New York City's South Street Seaport. There, standing on a small circular platform, wearing a helmet with built-in goggles and headphones and sheathing one hand in an electronic glove, I played the game *Dactyl Nightmare* on the Virtuality system, one of the first mass-marketed applications of VR. In an article Tracy wrote in 1992 for *Tricycle: The Buddhist Review,* she described what it was like for her to play this game:

> I gaze up at a galaxy of cartoon stars. Turning my head to the right, I see five checkerboard patterns linked by staircases and studded with simple geometric pillars and arches. Pressing a button on my hand control, I "fly" toward this gameboardlike space station, zooming closer and closer until I'm "walking" on an upper platform. Human and inhuman enemies are hiding.
>
> Darting around, weightless, in a bare, bright, mechanically uniform world, I try to steady the cartoon gun extended in the cartoon hand before me. The scene shifts with my gaze, though there's a tiny perceptual lag that makes me feel like I'm trying to focus underwater. A geometrically muscular cartoon man in blue pants appears. I squeeze the trigger on my hand control. Rocket grenades fall in slow white arcs.
>
> "Time to die," intones a cold computer voice. Amidst booming quadraphonic heartbeats, squawks and screams, I try to aim my gun but a huge, lime-green cartoon shadow descends and engulfs me. The pterodactyl sweeps me higher and higher into space until I explode into brightly colored confetti. . . .[2]

Playing *Dactyl Nightmare,* I became intensely aware of the movements of my body through the "real" world, and of myself trying to control those movements, because every small motion I made in the real world was magnified in the three-dimensional reality I was perceiving through the goggles and headphones. What I considered a small shift in my gloved hand caused my virtual hand, holding the gun, to swing in a wild arc. The experience was a bit like looking in a mirror while trying to direct your mirror hands to fasten a bow tie or to pin a brooch; the mirror hands seem all thumbs, casting into sharp relief both your more adept real-world hands and your mind as it tries to reconcile the two realities.

Jaron Lanier, the entrepreneur-scientist who coined the term "virtual reality," said in an interview in a subsequent issue of *Tricycle*, "The experience of virtual reality forces you to notice your own experience of consciousness.... By noticing the sharp-edged boundary of the objective world in VR, you also notice that there is something on the near side of that boundary."[3] My experience is that this is true, but only at first. I haven't played *Dactyl Nightmare* again, but by now I've logged hundreds of hours online, and when I sit in front of my computer screen I find that I lose contact with my body as quickly as I do when watching TV.

Ironically, a number of the pioneers and shapers of cyberspace are concerned about its power to sunder us from the natural world. Thomas Zimmerman, who as a young MIT graduate invented the DataGlove—the prototypical virtual-reality glove—told Tracy in an interview that VR "drives you up into your head. There's a heavy emphasis on external stimuli, on visuals and sound. What it's doing is enhancing the *dukkha* [the Buddhist term for the suffering that is said to pervade all existence], even though it is interactive. It appeals to the excited mind rather than to the contemplative mind."[4] Mitch Kapor, designer of the popular software application Lotus 1-2-3 and cofounder with John Perry Barlow of the Electronic Frontier Foundation, has expressed similar concerns, while in a recent issue of *Utne Reader,* Barlow asks about virtual communities, "What is missing? Well, to quote Ranjit Makkuni of Xerox Corporation's Palo Alto Research Center, 'The *prana* is missing,' *prana* being the Hindu term for both the breath and spirit. I think he is right about this and that perhaps the central question of the virtual age is whether or not *prana* can somehow be made to fit through any disembodied medium."[5]

Cyberspace draws us in large part because it feeds our restless desire for change, allowing us to experience a mock transformation. Even now, as I type, my eyes wander to the shelf where my copy of *Star Wars' Rebel Assault* sits. In ten seconds, by sliding the game disk into my computer's CD-ROM drive and clicking my mouse a few times, I can forget that I'm Jeff Zaleski, and can play the role of Rookie One, ace spacecraft pilot, weaving my way through a storm of asteroids, navigating my craft at warp speed as I fight at the side of Luke Skywalker to defeat Darth Vader and the Empire. Through games like *Rebel Assault* or *Doom,* in which the player adopts a new persona, and through the pseudonymous handles so prevalent in online communication, cyberspace feeds the same organic hunger for transformation that has children playing games of dress-up and make-believe. But does the present-day content of cyberspace—the games, the conversations, the databases that fill it like ether—offer any possibility of real transformation?

I know that certain works of art can enliven us, awakening us to the cosmos and our place in it. I think of two *lohans,* ceramic statues of meditating Buddhist monks, fashioned by anonymous craftsmen and now sitting in the Metropolitan Museum of Art. These *lohans* can be felt to emanate a living presence, one that vibrates with and intensifies one's own sense of presence. I think also of the power of music, of Gregorian chant and of Bach and The Beatles. Curious whether others' experience of art corresponded to my own, I posted a question about this on ECHO. The first response I received was from "Grey Zone 1," who replied:

> I was a white-trash art illiterate wraith who at age, I dunno, really young walked into a museum, saw two paintings by Kandinsky, his more geometric abstract phase, and I broke into tears. Everything that was anything was in these paintings.
>
> All The Beatles records when I heard them as a kid transfixed me in a way that was far beyond mere listening pleasure. Still do—it's weird. Beethoven's 7th—Second Movement. The books of Philip K Dick. *Dandelion Wine* by Ray Bradbury. Tales of Hoffman. An installation by Aimee Morgana. All changed me forever.

Grey Zone 1 posted that message at 2:39 A.M. on the morning of January 28, 1995, a Friday (online devotees tend to keep late hours). Shortly after midnight on the following day, wanting to elaborate on how the music of The Beatles had influenced his spiritual growth, he entered this amazing follow-up, edited here for length:

> This may sound goofy—but I think there exists no better analogue for an argument in favor of a "divine force, God, whatchamacallit" than The Beatles.... I know of which I speak. Mainly—sound. For fifteen years, I was a professional musician/engineer/producer/writer/whatever. The more I learned about the primary, physics-related, hard-ass science aspects of music reproduction, the more in awe I grew of the formation called The Beatles. Why?
>
> Simple. What they did was impossible. Really—several laws of probability—chaos and just plain common sense were blithely broken by these four guys (and George Mar-

85

tin). Lets take the simple miking of a drum. Today ... [all] this expensive stuff is used (and it takes hours, hours JUST FOR ONE DRUM!) to get a sound inevitably inferior to, say, Ringo's snare.

Now, imagine how long it takes and how much gear is used to get a guitar sound. A complete vocal. To mix the entire thing.... The point is, The Beatles, armed with a couple of compressors, a recording console that makes your stereo look like the Millennium Falcon, and some *very* old mics, INEVITABLY, in a matter of HOURS, at the most DAYS, created records that for pure sonic inventiveness ... leave current product in the dust.

I am here to testify that as an excellent engineer with superlative ears (no brag—this is important), as a guy who has spent A YEAR on a single record at a multi-multimillion-dollar studio, and on the single, did 2,500+ computer-assisted remixes—I'm here to unequivocally state that ALL The Beatles records are simply flying in the face of every law of sound that exists....

"Take your secular, Intell-analogous secular brain—play The Beatles—request: explain. You will explode.

I recently listened to "And Your Bird Can Sing." Several times. The guitar and vocal sound, the mix....

Who needs church?

Grey Zone 1's Beatles posting inspired a long train of responses from several other ECHO members, which concluded with the following posting from "Questione'er," also edited for length:

...I absolutely concur about The Beatles. My first record was the American release ... of "Rubber Soul." I mean, from the age of five, I would sit, transfixed, at my family's upright piano, with the key cover down, mutely playing "air keyboard" to "You Won't See Me" and "It's Only Love" and of course that amazing Bach fugue sample that George Martin added to "In My Life." There was something about that music that got right to the core of me, and it was many years before it even occurred to me to buy any other records....

Though a computer game like *Rebel Assault* uses music to enhance its visuals, I have never found that it, or any other computer game—or in fact any other information that has come to me through cyberspace—had "got right to the core of me," as Questione'er said Beatles music had for him. Given this, I wondered again, and even more forcefully, about the spiritual implications of the cyber experience.

I thought that Stacy, with her vast online experience, might shed some light on the matter, so I asked her to meet with me to talk about my questions. As we conversed over strong coffee in a West Village café, classical music played in the background. Listening to it, I realized that Beatles music, and the music we were hearing, had been intended by its creators to be listened to by the whole organism, body, mind, heart, and soul, within the context of the natural world. Even film, which since 1930 has been dependent on music for its effects and is arguably the most emotionally powerful media yet invented, doesn't attempt to substitute a virtual world for the natural one; virtuality requires interactivity, the illusion of participating in an alternate world, and film is a passive media. The reality available in cyberspace, however, by inviting us to move through it, cleaves us from the natural world, and deliberately so; and without the natural world's *prana* to work through, as John Perry Barlow pointed out, can its art move our souls?

Despite my reservations about cybercommunications, I had noted in many of the more conversational postings on

ECHO an unusual freedom of expression. I knew that Stacy was writing a book, *The Electronic Mask,* that would deal with this phenomenon, so I asked her about it.

"Some masks conceal," she said, "and some masks reveal. People at Carnivale are famous for being completely free when they wouldn't be normally, because the mask liberates them. Something happens online. There, you get just enough anonymity to feel safe to reveal your inner self. You feel like you're invisible.

"Psychologists say that unburdening the soul and opening up is a positive experience. I tend to be the same way online that I am in person, and I'm very private. But I've seen people opening up online, saying such intensely personal things, that it almost makes me uncomfortable. When they talk to me at the Art Bar [where ECHO members meet face-to-face every other week], though, they always say that they are glad that they did."

As Stacy and I got into our own conversation, I found myself comparing our communication in person, or face-to-face (or "f2f," as it is referred to by veteran cybernauts), to our communication online. Sending messages back and forth to each other on ECHO, our exchanges had been fast and crisp and to the point. But in person, I noted that, at least on my part, a certain hesitancy set in. Though we'd split up over ten years ago, I felt our shared history sitting at the table with us like a third party—in the real world, real-world memories intruded. Seated across the small wooden table from Stacy, the richness and ambiguity of face-to-face communication became clear: the impact of a glance away or a direct stare, the subtle play of body language, the shadings of tone and pitch of voice, the wordless messages of smiles and laughs and frowns—all missing in cybercommunication, as was the most important element of all, the simple organic presence of another's body.

I asked Stacy what it was like to finally meet someone face-to-face after a long-standing relationship with them online.

"It's very awkward," she said. "It's awkward to have an incredible intimacy of the heart and mind and to have no knowledge of the flesh. You're embarrassed. 'Oh, god,' you might think, 'I said too much. This person is a stranger.' You literally have to get reacquainted in the flesh. This happens a lot faster as a result of the online experience but you still can't bypass the face-to-face experience."

In addition to the emotional openness I had noticed on ECHO, I'd also been impressed by a generosity of spirit, of people wanting to help one another. What did she think about this?

"It demonstrates dramatically how people are aching for this kind of connection," Stacy replied. "I've discovered in my own life, for instance, that people want to do good, that they want to do nice things, but that they don't really know where or how to start. But if you go up to them and say, 'Do this, this is a good thing,' they will always say. 'Yes.' Or if you ask, 'Can you do this for me?' they always say, 'Yes.' It's as if people are waiting to be asked. Online, there are endless opportunities to be kind. On the other hand, people can be just as vicious. When you break down inhibitions, you see equal amounts of kindness and viciousness. It liberates both.

"Regarding your question about the spiritual implications of online communication, people often want the big story, the big answer. But the important story, the important answer, is usually so simple, so small, like the fact that people can talk together every day. That may end up as being the important element in online communities. That's what people come back to."

Elaborating on the potential of online interactions, Stacy pointed out that when anyone goes online, they meet many kinds of people, including some, such as racists, whom they might feel an initial revulsion toward. "But because this person is not in front of you," she explained, "you can look at them and see how they feel, and get over the revulsion, not to the idea motivating the person but to the person themselves. You recognize their humanity, that they may be a father, mother, brother, or sister."

But what about the addictive nature of online communication? Did Stacy believe, as some have warned, that we are heading for an era in which more and more of us are going to be sequestered in our rooms, avoiding firsthand contact with others as we communicate or fantasize through our computers? Her answer surprised me.

"Actually," she said, "the exact opposite happens. If you get online and people are interesting to you, it gets you out of the house more. If you talk to someone online and they interest you, you want to meet them. It's a natural inclination. People want to meet. People are looking for any excuse to get together, to have a face-to-face. This happens on an international level, but obviously more so on a local level. And that is why I think local communities are going to be the way of the future. Cyberspace is cool because it breaks down geographical boundaries, but it would not be cool if it broke down cultural boundaries. What's the point of being able to go anywhere, if everywhere is the same?"

The night before I'd met Stacy for coffee, I had posted a final query on the Into the Mystic conference, asking ECHO members their thoughts about the spiritual ramifications of online communication. The first to respond was "Wolf Angel (transfigurarique in lupum)," who wrote:

> 90 percent of life happens in our heads. we project, we embellish, we glorify, romanticize, minimize, elevate, criticize. in the beginning, i completely immersed myself in cyberculture and it became realer than real. and it's impossible to explain, it must be experienced. someone said that love is the illusion that one person is any different from the next. isn't spirituality linked to psychology? don't we choose, on some level, what to believe, especially when the belief is in something unprovable? and aren't these choices shaped by our inner lives, our collected experiences and so on?

Wolf Angel's posting was followed by several others. "Pro Forma" commented that "EVERYTHING is sacred, including cyberspace. This is one of the finest arenas of mind we have come up with yet … the more we communicate, the more we evolve," and, in a further posting, added, "I think we evolve on a daily basis. Karma ensures that." The next day, "jag" logged in with this posting:

> Wish I cd say I've logged on to Satori, connected to the Server of Knowledge & Dreams, or at least been sucked into my terminal like a VR Trooper to find cybermonsters & "kick some gigabutt!" Has not happened yet anyway.
>
> Transformations come slower. Like Pro Forma says, on a daily basis. An online persona takes shape. How do I fit in here, who am I when I can mask & reveal myself thru a keyboard & a screen which then returns human feedback? Do I belong? To which groups?
>
> The online space is a great place for learning & giving instruction, root functions of any sort of yoga. Sometimes it's like an oracle, ask a question get an answer. And often the tangent roads lead to the most fertile grounds.

It's *just* a lot of mental activity, but when minds connect there can be a ferocious energy. Collective unconsciousness awakens with an appetite. Wm Gibson—yeah,
he's too trendy to even mention now, but what the hell—
played with the idea of voodoo in the Net, & there was also
an article in an early Wired. The point is, we tend to think of
computers as cold, mechanical—but there's that magic electricity thing, electricity like blood—& who knows what be-
atific fevers course thru these wires?

Reading these postings, it occurs to me that while awakening to the presence of my body and the wider world isn't
possible for me when I am online and lost in my head, I find
myself in the same situation in the "real" world, where I
am nearly always asleep to the sacred in and around me.
While cyberspace may reinforce the rule of what Buddhists
call "the monkey mind," that rule need not be absolute, in
cyberspace or out of it. *Prana* may not exist in cyberspace
but, then, I never do either, not really. My body always rests
in the natural world, breathing in and breathing out; it's only
that I tend to forget that it exists. But it is possible, if very
difficult, to remember that the body exists, even while playing *Rebel Assault* or typing words onto a screen—being attentive to the breath can help. Right now, as I type these
words into my computer, I am sensing my breath flowing in
and out. I am sensing the upward suck of my dreaming mind
as well, and I know from past experience that in a moment
my attention will be lost to that mind. But I also know that
my attention can return to my breath, and so to my body,
and that I can begin anew to experience the world, moment
to moment.

Moreover, as jag points out, learning and giving instruction come easily in cyberspace, secondarily because of its

vast databases but primarily because of the willingness of most people online to share and to help out. Each of us moves along the spiritual path in fits and starts, stumbling here, falling there. By sharing our experiences, we can learn from one another—from those who are ahead of us on the path, from those behind, and from those alongside—and perhaps pick up our pace. In Buddhism, the community of people dedicated to following the Buddha's path is known as a *sangha*. In a way, at its best, an online community can be a kind of *sangha*. I worry about the hypnotic lure of cyberspace, but I cherish the moments of heart-to-heart opening that have come to me there.

Cyberspace is an ever-expanding world in which new resources appear and old ones disappear daily. It is anarchic, chaotic, and difficult to navigate. But it also contains a richness of information and personal contacts for those interested in transformation.

Spiritually oriented resources online divide into two basic types: discussions and files. Discussions include private e-mail, or electronic mail; Listservs, or mailing lists, in which mail on a particular subject is shared among any number of subscribers; sequential public postings in forums or conferences of the type featured on ECHO; and live "chat," in which you communicate through written messages with others in groups or one-on-one, in real time just as on the telephone. Files include documents, photographs, movies, audio recordings, and software.

The range of information online is staggering, and so is the range in quality. Online, you can download, or transfer from a distant computer to your home computer, esoteric Christian texts that, without a computer and modem, would require you to fly to Rome and cab to the Vatican libraries to access; or you can participate in a furious conversation about the spiritual fine points of Barney the Dinosaur. In general, the information available online that deals with spiritual awakening divides into material relating to established religions and more free-form material that can run the gamut from New Age manifestos to AA discussion groups to announcements of courses in mind expansion.

Because cyberspace can be confusing to a novice, perhaps the best way to approach it is by joining one of the large commercial services, such as America Online (1-800-827-3338), Prodigy (1-800-776-3449), or CompuServe (1-800-848-8990). Each of these services features forums on spiritual and religious subjects, as well as access to the Internet. The level of discussion and depth of information on these services tends to be shallow, however, so once you're comfortable maneuvering within them, the next step might be to join one of the smaller commercial services like ECHO (212-255-3839) on the East Coast or the Well (415-332-4335) on the West Coast, where discussion is more intimate and informed. These smaller commercial services also offer access, usually limited, to the Internet. Smaller still are the thousands of bulletin board services that dot the nation, some of which are isolated islands in cyberspace; others may be connected to one another through [echomail] networks, and still others may offer limited Internet access. The advantage to bulletin board services is that they may be devoted to a single subject: for example, the Tiger Team Buddhist Information Network (510-268-0102), which partakes of two Buddhist [echomail] networks, BodhiNet and DharmaNet, and offers its own forums and databases.

Then there is the Internet, the vast network of thousands of computers that are, for the most part, based at universities and other institutions. Resources on the Internet divide into four types. The most sophisticated are the Listservs, which can be accessed through any online service that offers Internet e-mail, as many services do. Most Listservs are moderated by an expert in the subject of the particular mailing list. Three of the best for those interested in transformation are Belief-L, which offers free-form discussion of personal religious beliefs and whose electronic address is listserv@brownnvm.brown.edu (it's centered in a computer at Brown University); OBJ-REL (listerv@emuvm1.cc.emory.edu), which offers discussion of topics such as the existence of God and epistemology; and SSREL-L (listserv@utkvm1.utk.edu), which is devoted to the scientific study of religion.

Similar in scholarly tone to the Listservs are the assorted databases on the Internet packed with files relating to religion and spiritual growth. These file sites, located at computers worldwide, are generally available through fewer of the online services than is Internet e-mail. Some of the more interesting ones are available on the World Wide Web discussed on pages 96 and 97.

Less erudite than Listservs or file sites, but often far more exciting, are the Usenet groups, generally unmoderated discussion groups that operate through sequential postings, much like the conferences on ECHO. Most online services offer access to many, often most, of the Usenet groups, which number about ten thousand. It is here that Barney the Dinosaur may be referred to as Barney the Avatar (on alt.religion.barney), but also here are many serious, if freewheeling, discussions bearing directly on questions of spiritual transformation. Among the more intriguing Usenet groups are alt.religion.all-worlds, alt.religion.gnostic, alt.religion.shamanism, soc.religion.christian, soc.religion.eastern, soc.religion.gnosis, soc.religion.islam, talk.religion.newage, and, for those who care, alt.religion.computers, alt.christnet.second-coming.real-soon-now, and the perennial favorite, alt.buddha.short.fat.guy.

Linking many of these sites is the World Wide Web, a navigational shell placed over the Internet that allows you to move from one site to another through hypertext, a web of key words that link one site to another. Not every site on the Internet has a Web site, or "home page," and as of this writing, Web access remains the least common of all forms of Internet access, although each of the three major online services, CompuServe, Prodigy, and America Online, now offer it. Spidering along the Web is the easiest way to move through cyberspace, as long as you're doing it with a graphical Web "browser" such as Mosaic, and many Internet sites, particularly commercial ones, are readily available only through the Web. There are hundreds of Web pages devoted to spirituality. The best way to begin to move through them is by logging on to a home page that lists myriad others like a table of contents. One of the most popular of these home pages is Yahoo (http://www.yahoo.com), a master table of contents to the Web. Once you reach the Yahoo home page, you can click on the highlighted words "Society and Culture," and, when the Society and Culture page appears on your screen, on the highlighted word "Religion." There you will find over one hundred spiritual categories listed, from "Avatar Meher Baba" through "Free Daism" to "Spiritual Leaders," and by clicking on each you will connect to a home page devoted to the appropriate subject or to another, more detailed listing (as of this writing, there are 56 home pages devoted to Judaism alone). The future of cyberspace lies along the World Wide Web and its nearly inexhaustible threads.

Finally, there is IRC, or Internet Relay Chat, at once the most intimate and, generally, least useful of Internet resources. This is the Internet's version of live "chat," a collection of hundreds of "channels," each demarked by a "#" sign and each devoted to a particular subject—for example, #zen.

Cyberspace is different from real space, yet it is also the same: If you enter it with attentiveness and an open heart, you may just find the information and connections you need to take you one step further along the path.

SCIENCE

"Let's consider your age to begin with—how old are you?"

"I'm seven and a half, exactly."

"You needn't say exactly," the Queen remarked. "I can believe it without that. Now I'll give you something to believe. I'm just one hundred and one, five months and a day."

"I can't believe that!" said Alice.

"Can't you?" the Queen said in a pitying tone. "Try again: draw a deep long breath, and shut your eyes."

Alice laughed. "There's no use trying." she said. "One can't believe impossible things."

"I daresay you haven't had much practice," said the Queen. "When I was your age, I always did it for half-an-hour a day. Why, sometimes I've believed as many as six impossible things before breakfast."

—LEWIS CARROLL,
Through the Looking-Glass

ONE SUMMER WHEN I WAS A BOY, I FOUND A DEAD SPAR-row in back of our Long Island house and decided to bury it. With a short-handled spade, I dug a hole in a corner of the yard, scooped up the bird, and dropped it in. As I re-filled the grave, the patter of dirt falling on the body sounded like a violation. Still, I finished what I had begun, said a prayer over the spot, and went to tell my parents about my good deed.

Two or three weeks later, for no particular reason, I decided to dig the sparrow up. I knew my parents wouldn't approve, so I kept my plan to myself and slipped outside long after dinner, in the dark. Carrying the spade and a flashlight, I walked across the grass and knelt at the grave. The blade slid easily into the earth and soon I felt the weight of the bird against it. A thrust of my arm and a flip of my wrist revealed the corpse.

It was covered with maggots—dozens, many hundreds, glistening white as they wriggled over bone and putrid flesh in the beam of the flashlight. I jumped back, disgusted. This wasn't the bird I had buried, a feathered beauty that had looked as if it still could rise up, spread its wings, and fly. This was some rotten *thing*. Averting my eyes, I scattered the dirt back over the corpse and ran inside. I told no one of what I had done and seen.

The memory of this event came back to me as I began to look into what science has to say about spiritual transformation. From media reports and my own reading, I knew that an increasing number of scientists have been exploring the intersection of mind and body. Physician Dean Ornish, author of best-selling books such as *Dean Ornish's Program for Reversing Heart Disease,* has conducted widely publicized studies demonstrating that meditation and group therapy can reverse arterial blockage. At the Stress Reduction Clinic that he directs at the University of Massachusetts Medical Center, Jon Kabat-Zinn has adapted Buddhist methods of mindfulness to help relieve patients of their chronic pain. And Candace Pert, visiting professor at the Center for Molecular and Behavioral Neuroscience at Rutgers University, has done breakthrough work linking the mind and the body through the messenger molecules known as neuropeptides.

Clearly science has established a connection between mind and body—but to my surprise, I found that it has little to say about how we open to higher realms of experience. I also learned that many scientists seem to scoff at the spiritual, at least in their professional lives. As scientists, they view the soul as a mirage and believe that the mind, whether of a bird or a human, arises from the body and is melded to it like skin. When the body dies, the mind dies with it; nothing remains but a corpse, food for maggots.

> You, your joys and your sorrows, your memories and your ambitions, your sense of personal identity and free will, are in fact no more than the behavior of a vast assembly of nerve cells and their associated molecules.[1]

These opening words to Francis Crick's *The Astonishing Hypothesis: The Scientific Search for the Soul* state the position of mainstream science about as baldly as possible. Crick, who won a Nobel Prize in 1953 for his discovery of the molecular structure of DNA, means his book, published in 1994, to be a rallying cry for the scientific study of consciousness. "The aim of science," he writes, "is to explain *all* of the behavior of our brains, including those of musicians, mystics, and mathematicians"[2]—and including attention, thought, reason, emotion, creative response, the sense of free will, and mystical experience.

Is Crick's "Astonishing Hypothesis" correct? During a transforming moment, is that sense of a vital connection to the rest of life nothing more than a storm of neuronal activity? And if "I am the detailed behavior of a set of nerve cells,"[3] then why do my nerve cells sometimes create the sense of a sacred dimension to myself that isn't bound by space or time, that seems to be connected by love to the rest of the cosmos? In his book, which aims to explain consciousness by studying visual awareness, Crick doesn't venture into why nerve cells behave as they do, but elsewhere, other scientists have. The consensus among many is that any living being behaves the way it does for one reason: *survival*.

"We are survival machines," wrote Oxford University sociobiologist Richard Dawkins in his influential book, *The Selfish Gene,* "—robot vehicles blindly programmed to preserve the selfish molecules known as genes.... Much as we might wish to believe otherwise, universal love and the welfare of the species as a whole are concepts which simply do not make evolutionary sense."[4]

Sociobiology says that our genes set the biological pattern for our behavior. Underlying this principle is the theory of the "selfish gene." According to this theory—which is accepted by most professionals in the life sciences—genes, through natural selection, have programmed their carriers (for instance, our human bodies) to achieve one aim: the survival and replication of the programming genes. Behaviors that seem to connect us for reasons of the heart and the spirit—altruism, love, compassion—are really just masks hiding the naked face of the survival instinct. As Dawkins says, "my own feeling is that a human society based on the gene's law of universal ruthless selfishness would be a very nasty society in which to live. But, unfortunately, however much we may deplore something, it does not stop it being true."[5]

Confronted with these theories, it's difficult not to feel as if mainstream science has plunged us through Alice's looking glass. Yet I know that science can contribute to our sense of the sacred. Long ago, perhaps during the same summer that I buried the sparrow, I heard that one of our neighbors was going to set up a telescope on the sidewalk; all the neighborhood kids were invited to look through it. At the time, I was reading children's science fiction novels (*The Wonderful Flight to the Mushroom Planet* being my favorite) and dreaming about how, when I grew up, I would be an astronaut traveling to Mars and then beyond the asteroids. When I learned that the telescope was aimed at Saturn, I could barely contain myself as I waited on line with my brother Phil. At last I reached the head of the line and stood on my toes to look down through the eyepiece.

There it was, a pale yellow sphere encircled by a bright ring as unlikely as a halo. As soon as I saw it, my excitement turned to wonder. In that moment, I knew that science and its instruments could introduce me to marvels and enhance my sense of the miracle of existence—the very lesson I was reminded of during my initial forays into cyberspace. Why, then, does science sometimes seem so averse to the spiritual?

One apparent reason is historical. During the past four hundred years science has had to fight religious authority just to exist, and then to be listened to. The battle lines were drawn when Galileo dropped objects of varying weight from a height and noted that they fell to the ground at the same rate of speed, thus contradicting Aristotle and his "knowledge" that had been passed on century after century by Church authorities. The fight continues today in areas as diverse as gene-splicing and cosmology, and the upshot has been an understandable reluctance on the part of many scientists to take seriously anything connected with religion, and, by extension, the spiritual. Crick speaks for a great number of his colleagues when he writes, "If revealed religions have revealed anything it is that they are usually wrong."[6]

The second, more fundamental reason for science's general disregard of spiritual phenomena lies in how science works. The basic tool of science is the scientific method, which entails the gathering of information, then the application of logic to this information to come up with a hypothesis that can be tested by the gathering of more information through experimentation. Scientists collect information by observing—Galileo watching the objects fall—and to ensure that observations are more or less objective, measurement is required; in Galileo's case, measurement of the weight of the various objects and of the time it took them to fall. But this poses a problem regarding any scientific inquiry into the *experience* of consciousness. How can you measure a thought, an emotion, a mystical experience? You can't, of course. You can, however, measure the manifestation of these intangibles in matter—in the biochemistry of the brain, for example. It is only with the relatively recent development of neurobiology—which for the first time, permitted the measurement, in the brain, of a material manifestation of consciousness—that the biological sciences have considered the study of consciousness a worthwhile endeavor. During the middle decades of this century, even many psychologists considered the mind off-limits. What counted was what could be measured, and so behavioralism, which hoped to understand the psychology of the human organism strictly by measuring its physical manifestations, held sway in the nation's laboratories and universities.

The pitfall of relying on only what can be measured is highlighted in the assumption many scientists draw from cases of brain damage. We are all familiar with how a stroke can impair speech, sight, even the ability to reason. Crick devotes many pages to brain damage cases, even using them to pinpoint the site of free will in the brain: "Free will," he writes, "is located in or near the anterior cingulate sulcus."[7]

Perhaps; but a problem arises when, extrapolating from evidence that injury to the brain causes injury to the mind, scientists conclude, as many do, that brain gives rise to mind. This conclusion is refuted in *Recovering the Soul: A Scientific and Spiritual Search,* by physician Larry Dossey, cochair of the Panel on Mind/Body Interventions at the National Institutes of Health. Likening the brain to a TV set, Dossey points out that a "naive person" might reasonably assume that what he sees on the screen of the TV originates from inside the set. This person might believe this assumption proven, moreover, when, as he investigates the inside of the set, pulling out wires and transistors, the picture deteriorates, then disappears. "His 'proof,'" says Dossey, "parallels the logic of the brain mechanist who firmly believes that damage to the brain proves that that's where the mind originates."[8]

The teachings of every major religion dispute the idea that consciousness, or mind, originates from matter. When invited to respond to the comment that "scientists take the view that consciousness arises from a material cause," the Dalai Lama—a trained logician and amateur scientist whose hobby is the repair of antique watches—had this to say: "Matter can only be a cooperative cause, never the main or substantial cause for consciousness."[9] In other words, while matter may cooperate in the arising of consciousness by providing a material platform—the brain—from which consciousness can operate in our world, matter is not the primary cause of consciousness; that primary cause, at least according to the Buddhists, is mind itself, which they say is eternal and without cause.

What we apply our minds to, and how we apply them, has an impact on the body. The thirteenth-century Kabbalist Abraham Abulafia said of meditation on divine names:

After much movement and concentration on the letters [of divine names] the hair on your head will stand on end ... your blood will begin to vibrate... and all your body will begin to tremble, and a shuddering will fall on all your limbs, and ... you will feel an additional spirit within yourself ... strengthening you, passing through your entire body....[10]

A relatively few scientists, like Larry Dossey and Jeremy Hayward, the nuclear physicist who elicited the comment from the Dalai Lama, have been performing exciting research into the spiritual—as distinct from medical or psychological—implications of the intersection of mind and matter. The best known of these scientists are the physicists, such as David Bohm and Fritjof Capra, who are attempting to reconcile the insights of quantum physics and relativity to the insights of Eastern religion. Bohm has reinterpreted the ancient idea of the interdependency of all that exists in his conception of the universe as a hologram, the smallest fraction of which contains all the information embedded in the whole. In biology, pioneering research into the spiritual dimensions of consciousness has been conducted by medical researchers like Dossey, whose most recent book, *Healing Words: The Power of Prayer and the Practice of Medicine,* explores the effects of prayer on healing. Connections have even been made between the brain's chemistry and mystical experience. Neurophysiologist Peter Fenwick, senior lecturer at the Institute of Psychiatry in London and a man who does not believe in the absolute dependence of the mind on brain, related with a twist of irony at a talk given to the World Goodwill Forum in London in December 1993: "A man once came to me and said, 'I've lost my soul, and I've lost the finer part of myself, I can't understand things. I can't understand finer emotions. It's gone, and with it, my spirituality. It's all gone.' And so I did a number of investigations; they were all normal until I did one which looked at the blood flow through the brain. This revealed that he had a shortage of blood flowing through his right temporal lobe. I suggest that that was why he had lost his soul. So if you are going to argue for a position of the soul in the brain, try the temporal lobe."[11]

The connection between spirit and body seems to be more mysterious than many suspect. As Larry Dossey points out in *Healing Words,* there is no invariable correlation between spiritual attainment and good health: "Saints and mystics may be high spiritual achievers but may have poor physical health," while "people with little spiritual sensitivity—so-called spiritual reprobates—can enjoy extremely good physical health."[12] It has always struck me that so many of the Dalai Lamas died young, or that a number of great spiritual adepts, like Chögyam Trungpa, Rinpoche, who helped disseminate the ideas of Tibetan Buddhism in the West, suffered from psychophysiological afflictions like alcoholism. For all the well-intentioned and beneficial research on the relationship between mind and body being done by Dean Ornish, Jon Kabat-Zinn, Candace Pert, and others, for all the forums and conferences that Buddhists, Vedantists, and others have held to bring together Western scientists and Eastern spiritual practitioners, the relationship between spiritual awakening and the body remains, as Dossey says in *Healing Words* "a great mystery.... I mean mystery in the strongest possible sense—somebody unknowable, something essentially beyond human understanding."[13]

This statement struck me as an unusual admission for a scientist. Wanting to know more about Dossey's ideas concerning scientific approaches to the sacred, I telephoned him at his home in Santa Fe.

"From my readings," I said to Dossey, "it seems to me that most scientists believe that science will eventually explain the mystery of consciousness, and therefore, the mystery of spiritual awakening. What do you think?"

"I think there are limits to science," Dossey answered in a light Texas drawl. "There is something that keeps receding when we try to get our hands on consciousness because when we do that we are trying to use consciousness as both a subject and an object. There's something crazy about that approach, and I use the word *crazy* deliberately. It's not rational to believe that we can use consciousness to focus light on consciousness. That's like using the tongue to taste the tongue or, as Alan Watts once put it, like trying to bite your teeth with your own teeth."

"But what is it about science," I asked, "that gives rise to these limits?"

"Everything that counts cannot be counted. Science is great at quantifying, the quantifiable. But it's very difficult to quantify what feels like consciousness. I think that most people who are working in the field of artificial intelligence, in neural networks, in the intermediary metabolism of the brain, in psychoneuroimmunology, don't get it. They don't understand, or seem to be aware of, what in the West has always been called the 'mind/body problem'—that is, the chasm that apparently separates what we call 'matter' from what we experience as consciousness. They ride roughshod over this problem, behaving as if there isn't any separation between what we call 'mind' and what we call 'matter.' They equate the two, and when they say they're investigating 'mind/body' relationships, they're really talking about brain/body relationships.

"There is a denial that a mystery even exists," Dossey added. "There is a complete disrespect for anything ethereal that we might attach to consciousness, something perhaps immaterial. I don't think the outlook is very optimistic for Western science to shed great light on the problem of consciousness when most of the scientists who are studying it deny that any problem exists."

I couldn't have asked for a better cue to introduce Francis Crick and his "Astonishing Hypothesis" into our conversation.

"Scientists like Crick," Dossey commented, "and, in general, those who study artificial intelligence, neglect certain bodies of evidence, which, if they honored them, would destroy their premises. Their bugaboo is nonlocal consciousness. If there is such a thing as mental or psychological or spiritual action at a distance, their theories instantly begin to leak. They want to make consciousness entirely a matter of brain and body, but as soon as you say that something can happen distant to the brain, you've gone beyond the brain.

"I really honor Crick's contribution to science," he continued. "But there are realms of experience, and even of data, that he will not bring to the table, and as long as he refuses to do that, he, like most of his colleagues, are going to remain stuck while trying to think about consciousness. Crick refuses to look at the experimental evidence for nonlocality. If he did, I think he would see in an instant that his hypotheses are hopelessly flawed. Nonlocal experimental evidence of consciousness is the watershed in twentieth-century mind science. It is the watershed, and he will not cross that line. But unless a scientist is willing to cross that line and engage nonlocal evidence for consciousness, there's no hope of understanding consciousness."

"Why," I asked, "do you think that so many scientists have a problem with this evidence?"

"There are fashions in scientific thought, and the blind spot now is action at a distance. This is the concept that I think causes most of the intellectual indigestion. Historically, the problem arose during the debate between Kepler and Galileo. Galileo was the senior scientist, Kepler the young upstart who said that the earth's tides were caused by the tug of the moon's gravity. Galileo, in order to expose what he considered the sheer silliness of this position, said, 'These are the ravings of a madman. Why, Kepler believes in action at a distance!' That tradition continues today."

But I had a question about Dossey's emphasis on evidence of nonlocality, because I didn't see why mind acting at a distance negated the possibility that our mind arises from our brain. Isn't it possible that the mind arises from the brain and then acts at a distance through some sort of wave or energy field, just like electromagnetism?

"That hypothesis," Dossey replied, "is a matter of faith, without a shred of evidence to support it. There isn't any evidence to support the manufacture of consciousness by brains, at least not that I know of. And I think energy models of consciousness are hopelessly inadequate. Consciousness does not behave like energy. All forms of energy get weaker with separation from the source. This is called the law of the inverse squared. Energy falls off with increasing distance. No experiment ever done in parapsychology or prayer work, for instance, has shown this to happen. Prayer and nonlocal effects of consciousness do not decay in strength with increasing spatial separation. This is a crucial observation.

"In addition, there's the observation, confirmed over a century in careful experiments, that you cannot shield the effects of consciousness. You can put people in a lead-lined box and the effects of the prayer get through as if the shielding wasn't there. This has been replicated in experiment after experiment. No one has been able to shield the effect. Again, energy doesn't behave like this. You can shield energy and energetic effects."

But if consciousness isn't a form of energy or matter, how can it affect matter? "If mind is nonlocal and my prayer ends up affecting someone else," I asked, "how does that happen?" Dossey's answer told me a lot about the pragmatic approach that underlies his thinking.

"I don't know how nonlocal events happen in the universe," he said. "I come back to the current bottom line, which is that they do happen. Even in quantum mechanics, where nonlocality was first demonstrated about twenty or thirty years ago by some experiments that practically nobody argues with anymore, if you ask physicists how this happens they tend to throw up their hands. I think we ought to demand no more of nonlocal theories of consciousness than we demand of the theories of quantum mechanics.

"I feel comfortable acknowledging that we don't know. But by golly, we do know that it happens. We know that consciousness manifests nonlocally, but that just pushes the mystery a little deeper. I imagine we'll get closer to the answer, but whether we'll actually penetrate the mystery, I don't know. I think we'll wind up with God. I say that semiseriously because what nonlocality implies is omniprescience, infinities in space and time. And what are you talking about when you use terms like this? Traditionally we've defined God, or divinity, or the absolute, or the Almighty as being omnipresent and infinite in space and time: Well, that's nonlocality."

Since Dossey had introduced God into the conversation,

I thought I'd ask him about meditation. Did he meditate? He did. Then what, I asked, did he see as the difference between his scientific investigation and his meditative investigations?

"The two words that come to mind," he replied, "are *control* and *manipulation*. That's what science must do, control and manipulate specific variables. In my meditative experience, I strive for the precise opposite. I try to empty and to rid myself of any manipulation. Rather than try to manipulate the universe, I try to let it speak to me. This is a rather divergent activity from what most scientists do in their daily work."

The self-emptying during meditation that Dossey spoke of reminded me of a question I had regarding prayer. "If I pray for someone and there's a positive effect," I asked, "is that the result of my mind working on someone else's mind or is that God at work? In other words, is this simply a form of telepathy, or is there a greater or universal mind involved?"

"A number of people," Dossey answered, "say that prayer is nothing more than psychokinesis. Don't smuggle in God. But I think prayer does involve the absolute because I don't make any distinction between the small mind and the big mind, ultimately. To say that your consciousness might be able to affect somebody at a distance is for me to say that God did it. I think the concept of the divine within is real. I think that your mind is part of the larger universal absolute. It is not belittling God to say that your consciousness initiated a prayer event.

"We're never going to get anywhere in our understanding," he emphasized, "if we continue to say that God is up there totally disassociated from us, like some sort of communications satellite. I don't think that works because there is no travel time involved with prayer. Prayer isn't a matter of signals. It's a nonlocal event that is instantaneous. If God is omnipresent, God must be within you."

I asked Dossey if he had any final words. He took the opportunity to offer some reconciling comments about science.

"In his book *A Sense of the Cosmos,* Jacob Needleman made the point that science began as a spiritually transformative endeavor. In the 1600s, Newton and Bacon and others wanted to have an unmediated confrontation with reality. If that isn't a spiritual agenda, I don't know what to call it. They wanted to stop taking the Church's word for how the world was supposed to work, to not go through anyone to, as Needleman put it, 'go to the wall of truth.' So the earliest impulse in science was, I think, deeply spiritual. Needleman goes on to say that within a generation or two science had become the new dogma. The impulse, noble and spiritual as it was, was lost.

"Teilhard de Chardin (Jesuit paleontologist and author of *The Phenomenon of Man*) said that 'research is the highest form of adoration.' If you really do it right, science can be a spiritual path. The way science is practiced these days, it's far from a spiritual path—but in its highest form it can be transformative."

> *When I heard the learn'd astronomer,*
> *When the proofs, the figures, were arranged in columns before*
> *me,*
> *When I was shown the charts and diagrams, to add, divide, and*
> *measure them,*
> *When I sitting heard the astronomer where he lectured with much*
> *applause in the lecture-room,*
> *How soon unaccountable I became tired and sick,*

Till rising and gliding out I wander'd off by myself,
In the mystical moist night-air, and from time to time,
Look'd up in perfect silence at the stars.

—WALT WHITMAN,
When I Heard the Learn'd Astronomer

Perhaps there *is* a mystery that science finally can't penetrate. Consider, for example, what science has to say about one aspect of a spiritually transforming moment—its relation to memory. Tracy and I have noted that moments of awakening are engraved in the memory. A while ago, I came across a passage in the book *Gentle Bridges: Conversations with the Dalai Lama on the Sciences of Mind* that confirmed this observation. There, Robert B. Livingston, a neuroscientist, explains that "to be remembered, an experience must evidently be related to personal feelings."[14] When an experience carries an emotional charge, Livingston says, the hippocampus region of the brain orders the brain stem to store as information about the moment of the experience "whatever patterns were obtaining in the brain at that moment."[15]

In December 1994, *The New York Times* carried an article by Daniel Goleman on new findings about the biochemistry of emotionally charged memory. According to Goleman, an experiment carried out at the Center for the Neurobiology of Learning and Memory at the University of California at Irvine had implicated the body's "flight or fight" reaction, which is brought about by the release of the hormones adrenaline and noradrenaline into the bloodstream, in the "power of emotion-arousing events to sear a lasting impression in memory."[16] Goleman explained that whenever we have an experience that carries an emotional charge, a nerve running from the brain to the adrenals triggers the secretion of the two hormones; in turn, the hormones activate receptors on the vagus nerve, which activates neurons within the amygdala area of the brain, which then signals other brain regions to increase the impress of memory.

So now, through science, I know something more about how the body's biochemistry creates memories of events that touch my heart. But while science has increased my knowledge about these memories, it hasn't increased my understanding of them; it hasn't told me anything about the personal meaning I ascribe to my memories, about the particular "taste" of them in my mind. Our subjective sense of meaning—the response of our inner self to what is happening in us and around us—lies at the heart of any experience, and science, with its emphasis on measurement and logic, simply cannot plumb the mystery of subjectivity.

Logic seems a poor way to experience ultimate reality. Logic implies duality, differentiation, and separation, but spiritual truth tends toward wholeness. The great Hasidic mystic the Maggid of Mezerich said of prayer:

> Think of yourself as nothing and totally forget yourself as you pray. Only remember that you are praying for the Divine Presence. You may then enter the Universe of Thought, a state of consciousness which is beyond time. Everything in this realm is the same—life and death, land, and sea....
>
> You cannot reach this level if you are still attached to the physical, worldly things, for that means you are linked with the division between good and evil, the dualism included in the seven days of Creation. How then can you expect to approach the realm where absolute unity reigns?[17]

VISIONS OF MARY

THE SUN WAS SETTING WHEN JEFF, ALEXANDRA, AND I walked into Joseph Januszkiewicz's backyard, but the Virgin Mary wasn't due to appear until after dark. The June air was warm, sweet with the scent of roses. As the sun slipped away, it streaked lavender and molten pink and orange across the sky, as if heralding the approaching miracle.

The scene that confronted us on the lawn of the tan ranch house in Marlboro, New Jersey, looked like a cross between an open-air concert and a revival meeting. More than five thousand people sat waiting in rows on blankets and aluminum lawn chairs. They fingered rosaries and talked and stared at the sky above the little shrine that stood just off the back patio. It was there, above a stand of blue spruce trees, that Januszkiewicz had first seen the Virgin Mary. The very air and the sky seemed to carry the hope that tonight would be the night that they too might at least see a sign in the sky, some spark or flare or ghostly outline to hold as proof that she was really there, watching over them.

They looked like the sort of people you'd see in a suburban mall, young couples in stonewashed jeans, groups of retired ladies in crayon-colored sweatsuits with caps of permed white hair, a few burly guys with tattoos. Jeff and I guessed that most of them were regulars at the visitation site because they had come armed with coolers and vinyl picnic hampers. Everybody wore grave, rapt expressions and talked to one another in low, excited voices, the way people talk outside funeral homes and other places where they sense they're in proximity to great and mysterious happenings.

By the time we spread our blanket on the grass, the sunset had faded and the sky was turning that bottomless, celestial blue that precedes darkness.

"You heard what happened last night, didn't you?" an old lady asked her companions in the row in front of us. "The moon split in two."

"We didn't hear about that," said another woman. "But last time we saw a big colored ring spinning around the sun." She made sweeping circles with her hands.

Darkness fell. Minutes later, a swarthy, middle-aged man with a voice like a union shop steward stepped out on the patio and led the crowd in repetitions of Hail Marys and Our Fathers. After an hour, the raspy voice fell silent and Januszkiewicz, diminutive and grey-haired, hurried out of his house as he had on the first Sunday of every month for the past several years. Kneeling before the shrine, he sank into silent prayer.

The corresponding silence in the crowd was deep and genuinely touching. Twenty minutes later, Januszkiewicz said his first and only words, a quick recital of the Lord's Prayer, and rushed back into the house. Though he'd said nothing about whether he'd seen the Virgin Mary or what she may have told him, as soon as the door closed behind him pandemonium erupted.

"Look, look, over there! Do you see it? It's showering gold!" A scream and another scream, and hundreds of flashbulbs started popping off, aimed at the TV antennae over the house, at the blue spruce trees, at the stars. "Look at that planet. See it move?" I had come to Marlboro expecting emotional displays of piety but I was stunned by what was breaking out around me. These people wanted to see Our Lady, spinning suns, burning bushes, heavenly hosts, something—anything.

"That's heat lightning, over there, where she was," shouted a man, pointing toward the bursts of camera flash over the house. "That never gets reported by the press."

Far in the back rows, an old woman prayed in Italian with her arms stretched out like a cross, her palms open to the sky, the way ancient Christians must have prayed. She looked ecstatic and beseeching and oblivious, and she seemed emblematic of the yearning that gripped the crowd.

In recent years, there has been an eruption across the United States of sightings and other miracles involving the Virgin Mary. I have investigated three of them. In addition to visiting the apparition site in Marlboro, which appeared to Januszkiewicz only after he made a pilgrimage to Medjugorje, the mountaintop village in Bosnia where six visionaries have been receiving messages from the Virgin for more than a decade, I went to see a Coptic Orthodox Church in Bensonhurst, Brooklyn, where a copper icon of the Virgin was reportedly weeping oil tears. In suburban Lake Ridge, Virginia, I tried to track down an even rarer phenomenon. There, at St. Elizabeth Ann Seton Catholic Church, a young assistant priest, Father James Bruse, had developed stigmata—the bleeding wounds of Christ—on his wrists, feet, and chest. In his presence, said the faithful, statues of the Virgin Mary wept, people were healed, and rosaries turned from steel to gold.

Americans tend to believe in miracles, at least privately, and visions of religious figures have always appeared here, just as they have in villages in Europe. Yet to visit a public Marian site like the monthly event in New Jersey is to witness a widespread and passionate wish for religious experience, for firsthand contact with the divine. What is especially poignant at Marlboro, as at other sites, is the spectacle of thousands of people identifying with a single visionary. To an outsider, it is like watching people who are hungry filling themselves up by pretending to eat.

What was behind this recent surge in sightings, and this scramble for instant, dramatic contact with the divine? To find out, I spoke with several experts in Marian visions, beginning with Sandra Zimdars-Swartz, a professor of religion at the University of Kansas and author of *Encountering Mary: From La Salette to Medjugorje* (Princeton University Press, 1991).

"I think there's a general disillusionment with institutions these days," said Zimdars-Swartz, talking by phone from her home in Lawrence, Kansas. "People are disillusioned with everything from the scientific establishment to the Roman Catholic Church. In times like these, people tend to seek reassurance. That's what seems to be happening at these apparition sites."

Lex Hixon, author of *Coming Home: The Experience of Enlightenment in Sacred Tradition* and guide to a Sufi community in New York City, sees the American Marian phenomenon as an interplay between social and spiritual causes. On the one hand, he sees a conservative apocalyptic movement that is fueled by fears about the millennium, and by the press. But he also sees the appearance of these apparitions as evidence of a genuine opening to a higher intelligence to which many middle-class people in this culture have previously been closed.

"What I think of as the living water, a kind of stream of higher intelligence, could give rise to these apparitions," he told me. "It has an infinite nature. It includes the human psyche but isn't confined to it." According to Hixon, visions of Mary are springing up in middle-class communities around the country because our rationalistic bias against mystical experience is beginning to erode. "In the old days," he said, "in villages like Garabandal and Lourdes, apparitions would arise because there was a kind of spiritual openness or atmosphere of faith that would allow these underground springs to come up. In modern culture, we've laid a kind of parking lot over all of that, even inside our religious congregations. Lately, that parking lot has been dissolving because there's uncertainty all over the world, and these things are rising up again. Of course, we can't discount the role of the mass media in publicizing these events, but something much deeper is happening as well."

To find out what an authority of the Roman Catholic Church had to say about Marian visions, I turned to Father Benedict Groeschel, director of the Office of Spiritual Development for the Archdiocese of New York and author of *A Small, Still Voice,* a guide on evaluating reported miracles that was used by the Church commission that investigated the apparition at Marlboro. "I blame the sudden prominence and interest in this kind of phenomenon on the extreme rationalism in our culture," said Father Groeschel. "By emphasizing rationalistic explanations, contemporary theology has taken all the mystery out of the Bible."

A breakdown of this "extreme rationalism" may have contributed to the miracles in Lake Ridge, Virginia, a tidy Washington suburb whose residents drive BMWs with mobile phones and decorate the front doors of their neat colonial-style houses with wreaths of berries and twigs. The houses and lanes of this growing, affluent community have been planned and laid out with a military precision that seems at odds with the rolling Virginia landscape. Many who live here, including many of those who pour into St. Elizabeth Ann Seton Church to see Father James Bruse, are highly trained professionals who work for the military, the FBI, and the CIA, and who practice a simple, conservative brand of Catholicism that doesn't go in for the mystical. They fill their homes with state-of-the-art computers and folk art. Highly mobile, they idealize a rooted country life that has nothing to do with the high-pressure, transitory lives they lead.

It was here, in December 1991, that Father Bruse began bleeding from the wrists and feet. For months, few outside an inner circle of priests and Father Bruse's family knew what was happening. Bishop John Keating of Arlington, Virginia, asked Father Bruse's superior to have the priest quietly checked out by both a psychiatrist and an internist. Each judged Father Bruse to be normal. In March 1992, however, the gold-painted, fiberglass Madonna in the sanctuary of St. Elizabeth Ann Seton church reportedly began to weep in front of some five hundred people and Father Bruse's stigmata became public knowledge.

From that day to the present, thousands have descended upon the church hoping to see a statue weep or to receive a blessing from Father Bruse. Reports of miracles abound: The afflicted are said to have been healed, and others have witnessed the spinning suns associated with Mary since the sightings at Fatima. In the presence of Father Bruse, it is said, countless statues of the Virgin Mary have poured forth tears, including a tiny Madonna that was concealed in a woman's purse.

The balmy spring Sunday I attended mass at St. Elizabeth Ann Seton, the spare, modern church was overflowing with people hoping to see the four-foot high Madonna beside the altar weep or to catch a glimpse of the bandaged wrists of Father Bruse. When the mass was over, a small crowd flowed down the aisle to the altar and its Madonna with her artificial flower crown.

"She helps me feel God's presence," said one well-dressed woman from New Jersey who had been to Marlboro as well.

The Church hierarchy has withheld judgment on Father Bruse and the phenomena surrounding him. The Chancery of the Diocese of Arlington reacted to the events in Lake Ridge with a cautious statement: "In this particular case, there is no determined message attached to the reported physical phenomena, and thus there is no ecclesial declaration to be made at this time. As always in similar cases, the Church recommends great caution in forming judgments and advises against any speculation on the causes or possible significance of the reported events."

In other words, don't think about it. Many have, though, at least about apparitions in general, including Carl Jung, who considered Marian visions one of the "visionary rumors" that he claimed appear whenever a culture is poised for epochal change. According to Jung, these visionary rumors, or mass visions, are created by one or more visionaries gripped by an unconscious wish, fear, or fantasy that erupts from the unconscious in a concrete yet symbolic form that speaks to others so deeply that, in effect, it becomes real. The visionaries, Jung said, are those least able to accept the contents of their own unconscious. This theory may explain why Marian visions and other reported miracles are embraced with such fervor by those middle-class Americans who, like the residents of Lake Ridge, are faced with the herculean task of reconciling the rational, skeptical, conscious parts of their minds with their deeply emotional religious longings and fears. With no other outlet for the ecstatic or apocalyptic fantasies in their unconscious, when a symbolic projection erupts from a visionary like Father Bruse, they begin to share the vision.

"Personally, you couldn't get me to walk across the street to see a weeping statue. I'm also not very impressed by some of the stigmatics around," Father Groeschel of the Archdiocese of New York told me in his gravel-voiced, New York accent. "One must remember that interest in this kind of thing relates to humble people's religion. We have to have respect for the religion of the ordinary, humble person who, in a naive way, seeks to have his faith affirmed through tangible phenomena.

"People must try to put aside this childlike spirituality," he continued. "The great Christian mystics, for instance, were most concerned with personal religious experience, prayer, and the well-being of others. They were seldom impressed by this rather crude involvement in reports of extraordinary phenomena. Though some reports of miraculous phenomena are very impressive, they do not qualify for the highest level of spirituality."

Like Father Groeschel, Lex Hixon believes that the impulse to reconnect with the mystical should be honored, but that those enraptured by Marian visions need to grow and to question.

"The people you describe at Marlboro are getting a glimpse of the ancient Christian and Muslim ideal of the exaltedness of humanity," Hixon said to me. "But people have to move beyond the thrilling experience of looking up at the night sky and throwing their arms open wide and praying and feeling like they're directly in contact with the divine. Not to dismiss the fervor, but there's something very immature about it. It's a kind of spiritual puberty. People need to go further and learn to develop themselves so they can go help heal the earth and the rest of humanity. That's why we need the Bible and the Church and the liturgy and all the world's great religious teachings. You can't get the kind of instruction you need to develop spiritually just by standing in a field."

On March 21, 1994, New York City's ABC *Eyewitness News* ended with a shot of a pious tableau: a solemn, modestly dressed Egyptian immigrant family and their friends crowding an apartment in Bensonhurst, all of them staring up reverently at a glistening copper icon of the Virgin Mary. With detached amusement, the TV anchor announced that this icon, which the Boutros family had bought in a church gift shop in Cairo, had been weeping oil tears. The camera cut to an exotic, bearded figure in a long, black cassock, identified as a bishop of the Coptic Orthodox Church, a sect of Christianity centered in Egypt. The bishop assured the greater New York audience that a miracle had occurred.

By April, the icon was said to have stopped weeping, but the faithful continued to come to Bensonhurst's Coptic Church of St. George, where the icon now rested. Most, even the merely curious, crept up the aisle to the icon as if it were alive. These pilgrims would make the sign of the cross and stand reverently in front of the icon, a head fashioned of hammered copper and bowed down under an elaborate halo.

"We have the holy oil from the icon mixed with olive oil for the pilgrims," Father Mina Yanni told me on the day I visited the church. As I watched, visitors dipped balls of cotton into a jar of this mixture, a thick, greenish liquid carefully placed below the icon. Olive oil had been added to the icon's own secretions, Father Yanni explained, when the oil had stopped flowing.

"Of course it's a miracle," he proclaimed. "This is a message from St. Mary. She wants people to have good relations with the Lord." Father Yanni, a jolly, gray-bearded figure in black robes and a round black hat, added, "If it's not a miracle, how could the oil have gotten there? It's a message from St. Mary, who wants all people to be one."

The priest gestured toward a middle-aged woman with a wide smile who was standing in front of the icon. "Talk to her," he said. "She's Roman Catholic but she comes here every day."

"I can't help it. I love her. She's so beautiful," the woman told me, her accent vintage Brooklynese. Painted in gentle hues of blue and white and tan, the icon depicted the Madonna looming up between two church towers. Her gold halo and her pose, downcast in private supplication, looked Byzantine but her face was distinctly Western, as pale and delicate as that of a porcelain doll.

At the Coptic church in Bensonhurst, as I watched worshippers gaze in awe at the Madonna, it struck me that I was witnessing a religious version of the much-publicized "search for the inner child." In the presence of the icon, with its representation of the ultimate mother, compassionate and all-seeing, these faithful may have been "reparenting" themselves, releasing feelings of abandonment and abuse. In Mary's presence, they couldn't feel isolated or worthless or alone.

Father Yanni led me to his office, where he held out a notebook that contained handwritten accounts of personal miracles attributed to the weeping Madonna, including the amazing story of a man who experienced relief from the pain of his sciatica after he rubbed his back with a cotton ball dipped in the oily tears.

I pointed out the results of a recent test, conducted with the blessings of the Coptic Church itself before the flow from the icon had stopped. The "holy" liquid had turned out to be a form of vegetable oil. Could it be, I asked Father Yanni, that he had been the victim of fraud?

"I am not a victim of fraud," he told me. "I saw it with my own eyes. This was a miracle."

I wondered how many people in Bensonhurst and Marlboro and Lake Ridge were really open to the miraculous. At Marlboro and elsewhere, people tended to describe themselves as members of a movement, of a brave vanguard that stood for truth and light in a world of encroaching darkness. This identification of themselves as an army for Jesus Christ and Mary showed me that many were more interested in certitude and moral reassurance than in the kind of exploration that Father Groeschel said the great Christian mystics engaged in.

The desire for certitude—for our own proof of the reality of the divine—is a natural inclination, and part of the initial motivation of any spiritual search. Yet it seems that in order to have a deeper vision of ourselves and the world, we must see our identifications—including our need for proof—so that we can pass beyond them and allow the mystery in. A good measure of the value of any spiritual group or teaching, I realized after Marlboro, may be whether it supports us in opening up to the mystery, or whether it closes us down.

But Thomas, one of the twelve, called Did'ymus, was not with them when Jesus came.

The other disciples therefore said unto him, We have seen the Lord. But he said unto them, Except I shall see in his hands the print of the nails, and put my finger into the print of the nails, and thrust my hand into his side, I will not believe.

And after eight days again his disciples were within, and Thomas with them: then came Jesus, the doors being shut, and stood in the midst, and said, Peace be unto you.

Then saith he to Thomas, Reach hither thy finger, and behold my hands; and reach hither thy hand, and thrust it into my side; and be not faithless, but believing.

And Thomas answered and said unto him, My Lord and my God.

Jesus saith unto him, Thomas, because thou hast seen me, thou hast believed; blessed are they that have not seen, and yet have believed.

—THE GOSPEL ACCORDING TO ST. JOHN, 20:24–29

Without physical proof of the risen Christ, Thomas would not believe; he would not accept the mystery of the resurrection on faith. Years ago, I read an article that suggested that by wanting to thrust his hands in Jesus' wounds, Thomas was expressing a need to feel rebirth in his own body. After Marlboro, I understood better the yearning to be full of experience rather than to undertake the challenge of standing empty. Faith, I came to see, may mean having an awareness that includes body, heart, and mind—but it may also mean being aware that I am part of a reality, a cosmos, that in its deepest reaches will always be unknowable.

As the Christian mystic Dionysus the Areopagite said long ago, "At the end of all our knowing, we shall know God as the unknown."

SURRENDER

THE SPIRITUAL HOME OF THE NEW YORK CITY BRANCH OF the Jerrahi Order, an order of Sufi dervishes, is a small green building nestled in the heart of chic downtown Manhattan.

Walking into this mosque from the hard-edged urban stylishness of the surrounding cafés and restaurants, as Tracy and I did one Thursday evening, is like walking into another world. The central room is immaculate and bare of furniture, its floor covered with Persian carpets, the walls decorated only with the name of Allah painted in green and gold on lozenge-shaped canvases. As in every mosque, in one corner rises an intricately wrought *minbar,* or pulpit; in another is carved the *mihrab,* the niche that angles toward the Ka'ba in Mecca. All is quiet, the hush broken only by the creak of slippered feet on carpeted wood. The call is clear: Be still, and bear witness to the love and compassion of Allah.

The mind has its own agenda, however, and that night mine had locked onto a superficial concern: Would I be able to blend in with the others? Though I had never been to a mosque before, I knew that the evening's activities would include prayer. I don't speak Arabic, the language of Islam, and I was worried that my silence during prayer would make me stand out and be noticed. I decided to watch from the sidelines.

But the spiritual guide of the mosque, Sheikh Nur al Jerrahi, an American introduced in the previous chapter under his birth name of Lex Hixon, had a different plan for me. I heard him enter the mosque before I saw him. He greeted and blessed people, his voice swirling around his followers like water rushing over stone. When he saw me, the sheikh, an ebullient bear of a man whose white hair belies a boyish face that radiates light, stretched out his arms and smiled. "There you are!" As Sheikh Nur al Jerrahi embraced me, the dervishes—a mix of Arabs, Persians, African-Americans, and white Americans—began to line up in rows to pray, the men in front, the women behind. I was still hoping to slip off to the end of a row when the sheikh grasped my hand and led me to front row center. My self-consciousness went into overdrive.

I stood while the others prayed, and held my tongue. As the men beside me lifted their hands I followed suit, feeling as if I was playing a game of Simon Says in which everyone but me was Simon. When they lowered their hands, I imitated them. I managed to keep pace, if at a lag, but my mind was so caught up in not making a mistake that I might as well have been home watching TV: Nothing was getting through.

Everyone fell to their knees and touched their foreheads to the floor. Fascinated by this dramatic gesture, I did the same, and something remarkable happened. My body *recognized* the position it found itself in—and yet I'd never before prostrated myself during a formal act of worship. Wonder filled me, and gratitude. Prone on the carpet, my knees, forehead, and palms pressed against the floor, I sensed myself in an active relationship to the sacred, and knew that it was right. This feeling came back when all the dervishes were prostrating themselves seemingly as the spirit moved them. I felt not just a desire but a need to fall down on the carpet again and again, to express my obeisance to the divine and to remain prone for several seconds at a time. At no moment did I think, Now I'll prostrate myself. My body was obeying a command that came from somewhere deeper than my mind.

The next day, I marveled at how prostrating had quieted my mind, allowing my heart to speak. The body itself seems to contain knowledge about the sacred, I thought. It seems to know innately how to behave in the presence of the unknown.

I remembered what Tracy had told me about how she sank to her knees on the night she was mugged. As she stared up at the light that gazed down upon her, kneeling had felt natural and right. She had felt a little like one of the shepherds keeping watch in the fields the night Jesus was born, she'd told me, only she had been brought to her knees by the light of a holy star that had streamed out of her. I realized that my awakenings on the carpet in the mosque were further evidence that the wish for transformation is innate, a yearning written in the body. I had bowed just as I had learned to make love—as if I had always known how.

I remembered, too, that the word *Islam* is usually translated as "surrender" or "submission." What had surrendered the evening before, if only for moments? My upright stance, certainly, and perhaps the pride that goes with it, but something more. My worrying mind had given way, just as Tracy's calculating had when the mugger's arm tightened around her.

Surrender is integral to every transforming moment. To awaken, we somehow must surrender our attachment to the everyday mind, which like an infant usually demands all of our attention—right now! In a setting like a mosque, surrounded by worshippers, surrender can come without effort and may even seem necessary. In the midst of everyday life, it proves far more difficult. We are creatures of habit, barnacled to every aspect of our lives—our styles of dress, our friends, perhaps above all, as Gurdjieff said, to our sufferings. Anyone who has tried to diet or give up smoking, or who has lost a lover, knows how difficult letting go can be. The trouble lies not so much in giving up the object of our attachment—the lover is already gone, the nicotine has been withdrawn from—but in surrendering our image of ourselves as someone forever entwined with that lover, as someone who *is* a smoker, who *needs* that slice of chocolate cake—or, most common of all, who is a victim of life. How, in order to achieve transformation, can we then begin to surrender our ties to our lifelong companion and advisor, our personal secretary of defense: the chattering ego self that tells us how important we are and how good or bad the rest of life is in relation to ourself?

In fact we can't, at least not at will. Ego mind will never surrender of its own accord, and our trying to outwit it is like an alcoholic's trying to give up drinking while drunk. It just doesn't work. Yet transformation *is* possible, because the first step toward it doesn't depend on our ordinary self. The first step in a moment of awakening always comes to us as a gift, whether by ego mind being stunned into silence by a physical or emotional crisis, or whether through a call from a greater Self that breaks past our incessant internal commentary. We have a vital role to play in these moments, and we can, through training, learn to become more sensitive to them and to respond to them more intelligently—to learn better how to, as is said in Alcoholics Anonymous, "let go and let God." But we can't awaken at will; we are, in fact, *awakened*.

One of the most majestic examples in literature of how life can begin the process of awakening can be found in Shakespeare's *King Lear*.

By Act III, the aged Lear, who has given away his kingdom to his evil daughters, Goneril and Regan, has been cast out by them into a raging storm. Wandering in the wind and rain, Lear confronts his state:

> *Here I stand . . .*
> *A poor, infirm, weak, and despis'd old man.*

The king meets Poor Tom, a beggar shivering naked under a blanket. Looking at this sorry figure, the king begins to undergo a transformation: He is able to see mirrored in Tom his own naked self, hidden for so long behind royal robes. He sees himself without pretense and without defense: "a poor, bare, fork'd animal." The true nature of his ego—bestial, without dignity or intrinsic value—has been unveiled. Then Lear is struck one more blow, the death of his beloved third daughter, Cordelia:

> *Howl, howl, howl! O, [you] are men of stones!*
> *Had I your tongues and eyes, I'ld used them so*
> *That heaven's vault should crack. She's gone for ever!*
> *I know when one is dead, and when one lives;*
> *She's dead as earth.*

This is more than Lear can bear:

> *No, no, no, life!*
> *Why should a dog, a horse, a rat have life*
> *And thou no breath at all? Thou'lt come no more,*
> *Never, never, never, never, never.*

And so Lear dies, a broken man. Despite the torrent of blows that life rains upon him, despite his having seen the naked fragility of his ego self, Lear has not been able to let go of his ego and its demands completely. Until his dying breath, he reacts to the world and what it brings with howls of protest, insisting that it be this way rather than that—but life pays no attention to his wishes and breaks him over its indifferent knee.

Lear need not have perished. When a man or a woman reaches the end of their rope, they may hang themselves with it, as Lear did, but another choice is possible: to let go of the rope, to leap into the unknown. This is the leap of transformation. For centuries, scholars have been aware that Shakespeare modeled Lear on the biblical character of Job. In the Book of Job, we find a man whose ego, like Lear's, is flayed to transparency by life's blows—but who, at last, lets go and surrenders to a greater reality.

Job, the Bible tells us, has been a man "perfect and up-right, and one that feared God, and eschewed evil." But one day Satan approaches God and asks, "Doth Job fear God for nought?" Pointing out the wealth that God has given Job, Satan warns, "But put forth thine hand now and touch all that he hath, and he will curse thee to thy face"—to which the Lord replies, "Behold, all that he hath is in thy power." Satan afflicts Job with suffering upon suffering. Job loses all he has, even his sons. His relatives forsake him; his servants treat him like a stranger; he watches the wicked grow rich and live long. Finally, Satan plagues Job with agonizing boils.

Like Lear, Job rails against his sufferings. He proclaims his innocence and cries out for an explanation. "Oh, that one would hear me! behold, my desire is, that the Almighty would answer me, and that mine Adversary had written a book." God answers Job out of the whirlwind: "Where was thou when I laid the foundations of the earth? declare, if thou hast understanding." The Lord rebukes Job and refuses to account for his terrible fate. "Wilt thou also disannul my judgment? Wilt thou condemn me, that thou mayest be righteous?"

As God wears down Job's insistence on justice, Job comes to understand that he has been blind to the power of the divine, and to the mystery at the heart of the universe.

> I know that thou canst do every thing, and that no thought
> can be withholden from thee.
>
> Who is he that hideth counsel without knowledge?
> therefore have I uttered that I understood not; things too
> wonderful for me, which I knew not.
>
> Hear, I beseech thee, and I will speak: I will demand of
> thee, and declare thou unto me.
>
> I have heard of thee by the hearing of the ear: but now
> mine eye seeth thee. Wherefore I abhor myself, and repent
> in dust and ashes.

Unlike Lear, and like Ebenezer Scrooge, Job has relinquished his insistent self. Like Scrooge, he is pierced with remorse and can now see the world as it is, without reference to how it benefits him. And as with Scrooge, what follows for Job is joy, for the Lord "accepted Job. And the Lord turned the captivity of Job, when he prayed for his friends: also the Lord gave Job twice as much as he had before"—a gift that in typical biblical metaphor is presented as a bounty of sheep, camels, oxen, asses, sons, and daughters, but which we can read as the bounty of spiritual riches that comes to us whenever our ordinary mind gives way to the greater Self.

Not long ago, I heard someone speak words that echoed

the Book of Job's happy ending. I was trying to quit smoking and had noted that every Tuesday night a local church hosted a meeting of N.A., which I assumed stood for Nicotine Anonymous. The following Tuesday I walked to the church and followed signs to the meeting hall. There I realized my mistake, for on the wall hung a banner reading NARCOTICS ANONYMOUS. Even so, I decided to stay to see what I could learn. A half-hour into the meeting, a skeletal man of about forty, wearing a black hat with a wide floppy brim, began talking about the AIDS clinic he and his wife had started. Apparently they had launched this project with only their meager life savings. After a while, more funds flowed in, and now the clinic was a great success. "It's just like the program says!" the man exclaimed. "Give, give, and whatever you give will be returned to you tenfold." He made it clear that he wasn't referring just to the giving of money, but to the giving *up* of the attitude of self-interest, the parsimony of emotion, that had taken him down the road to addiction. He mentioned Step Three as the source of his inspiration.

Step Three is the third of the Twelve Steps in the many programs of recovery that began with Alcoholics Anonymous but that now include Narcotics Anonymous, Nicotine Anonymous, Overeaters Anonymous, and more. The first three steps read:

1. We admitted we were powerless over alcohol—that our lives had become unmanageable.

2. Came to believe that a Power greater than ourselves could restore us to sanity.

3. Made a decision to turn our will and our lives over to the care of God *as we understood Him.*

These steps offer a clear summary of the process of spiritual surrender. Though intended for alcoholics, they seem to apply to us all, especially if we substitute the word *life* for *alcohol* in the First Step. That step would then read, "We admitted we were powerless over life—that our lives had become unmanageable." Lear made this admission when he saw the body of his daughter, "dead as earth," but he never moved past this step. Job, too, came to see that he could neither fathom nor control his life, but unlike Lear, he came to believe in a "Power greater than ourselves"—a God whose motives lay beyond the reach of human reason. Job took the Third Step as well, turning his will and his life over to God.

In Manhattan's Greenwich Village, across from the gothic towers of the Jefferson Market Library, stands the duplex apartment that Donald Newlove shares with his wife, Nancy, and the 25,000 books that line their home floor to ceiling, room to room. A generous man with a wide grin, Don delights in the fact that the apartment is a converted speakeasy. The joke is that for the past twenty years he has been an active member of A.A., writing about his experiences with alcoholism and recovery in several acclaimed books.

Snow lay in mounds along the sidewalks of the Village on the day that Tracy and I visited the Newloves. Inside their home, warming up over coffee and munching from a plateful of cookies, we asked Don what it means to take the Third Step. After thinking for a moment, he emphasized that surrender doesn't happen all at once. "There are many moments of surrender," he said. "One builds upon the other." Pressed by our questioning, he suggested that we turn to his book *Those Drinking Days: Myself and Other Writers*.

In this book, Newlove describes his years as "Drunkspeare," a young writer of great promise but so besotten with booze and pot that while novel after novel chattered out of his typewriter, none were publishable. By the time Drunkspeare turned thirty-five, it wasn't only his writing that suffered:

> I was now almost two-hundred-and-fifty pounds, red-faced, losing my hair, given to cankers and bleeding gums ... I got dizzy rising from chairs or picking up a handful of spilled coins, must I mention ... the mental fog that had me leaning on the table trying to remember my middle name, my age or where I just laid down my glasses, my rage over a dropped spoon....[1]

By nearly anyone's measure, this qualifies as an "unmanageable" life. Yet even after Drunkspeare began to attend A.A. meetings, he continued to drink and smoke pot, in between spells of sobriety, until one day in Florida:

> I stiff-legged my body into the kitchen and ... poured two ounces of Ethyl into a waterglass and drained it. The booze bloomed through my shoulders, then fell like death-salts through my body. Every cell was stunned, my brain a gnarled fist of smoke. Death wavered within me like a second body. Self-insult and humiliation could go no deeper. I'd hit bottom.
> "That was my last drink," I said to my mother.
> And it has been.[2]

Instead of stepping to the liquor store, Drunkspeare began to take the steps. He finally realized that his life had, even by his own generous measure, "become unmanageable"—or at least unmanageable by him. But who would manage it?

> I was psyching myself for touching my unadmitted Higher Power and for three months a terrific cloud built in

me, so that everywhere I turned I saw signs and warnings, heard an inner whisper. . . . One afternoon, going down the hall from my kitchen to my study, my feet were swept back, I landed on my knees as if scythed, and found myself in a cloudburst of prayer. I hobbled into my bedroom and went on praying beside the bed, sobbing without stop.[3]

Newlove attended A.A. meetings for five years before he took the Second Step—though it might be accurate to say that the step took him. Life can bring us again and again to the brink of surrender. At some point, though, we have to participate in the process of letting go and of our own transformation. The Third Step is clear about this: *"Made a decision* [my emphasis] to turn our will and our lives over to the care of God. . . ."* For Newlove, this step seems to have come a day or two after his feet were swept back in prayer. As he lay in bed one night, agonizing over his inability to "escape" himself, the faces of all the men and women who had ever loved or helped him arose one by one in his mind. As they did, he blessed each until "I lay tearstained with openhearted prayer, no mask, no personality, only a direct pipeline of blessings from my Higher Power."[4]

Both Donald Newlove and Job suffered terribly before they were able to let go of themselves. Their stories are stories of surrender written large and with great drama. Yet on a smaller scale, we are each given the opportunity time and again, day after day, to undergo the same process of surrender and to play our part within it. Each rare moment in which we are awakened from the narcissistic dreams of our ego, we can participate: by blessing the awakening, by opening up to whatever it brings. We scarcely ever do, however. Nearly always, ego immediately steps in to comment on the experience, plunging us back into our dreams. We can, however, and in the rarest of instances do, respond to a movement of awakening with a movement of our own. This movement is one regarding the attention. We can choose to allow the attention to encompass whatever is before us in the moment, and thus permit the process of surrender, of opening, to take place.

Our relationship to moments of awakening seems akin to that of a gardener to her crops. She doesn't grow the crops herself—nature does—but she can prepare the ground and, when the crops arrive, tend to them. Similarly, through meditation and prayer, we can prepare our inner ground to provide receptive soil for a moment of awakening, and when one arrives, we can help it, through the attention, to take root and grow. If we do, we see that ego mind loses volume and force, albeit only for an instant: For the lower bows to the higher and ego mind will yield to the sacred if it is not fed by our attention. Inevitably and quickly, ego mind will rise anew and claim us for its own, pulling us into its fantasies and daydreams and melodramas; but in the next moment we can begin again, and in the next moment yet again. Perhaps every moment could bring us to wakefulness, if we only knew how to attend.

This vigilance of attention may be what Jesus meant when, in the garden of Gethsemane, he said to Peter, "Watch and pray, that ye enter not into temptation." It is the core of traditional spiritual training and practice, from the repetition of the Prayer of Jesus of the early Christian monks—"Lord Jesus Christ, Son of God, have mercy on me!"—to the whirling of the Mevlevi Sufi dervishes, from Hindu yogic exercises in one-pointed concentration to the mindfulness meditation of Buddhists.

Because our ego minds are so dominant and our attention so weak, it seems unlikely that we can, without guidance, make any sustained, effective effort toward surrender and awakening. The great religious traditions and the spiritual teachers in whom they are embodied can offer this guidance. One of the most powerful prayers ever given regarding surrender is the Lord's Prayer. No matter what our religion, or if we practice no religion or a combination of several, this prayer, given by Jesus during his Sermon on the Mount, can awaken us to the sacred within if it is recited carefully, with an open heart. It is useful, I have found, to sit quietly for a few minutes, coming to a sense of body, heart, and mind as a whole, alive in the world—and then to say the prayer, allowing each word to resonate within:

> Our Father, which art in heaven,
> Hallowed by thy name.
> Thy Kingdom come. Thy will be done
> in earth as *it is* in heaven.
> Give us this day our daily bread.
> And forgive us our debts, as we forgive our debtors.
> And lead us not into temptation, but deliver us from evil:
> For thine is the kingdom, and the power, and the glory,
> for ever.
> Amen.

—THE GOSPEL ACCORDING TO ST. MATTHEW, 6:9–13

TRADITIONS

ONE DAY I LEFT ALEXANDRA WITH JEFF IN BROOKLYN, took the subway to West 96th Street, and walked nine blocks north along Riverside Drive to visit the New York Buddhist Church. It was one of those warm, azure autumn days that edges everything with gold. As I walked, I was filled with vague thoughts about the swiftness of time—my daughter was in her last year of preschool, and a friendship I had once cherished was fading. I felt the tug of my attachments to people, objects, and ideas as a centrifugal force inside that kept me spinning, constantly deflected from the present. I wanted just to walk and take in the sights and sounds around me. I wanted to practice choiceless awareness, a total acceptance of what is; but as I tried, I became aware only of how closed I was—something in me kept turning back to memories and dreams.

The alchemy of seeing began to work on me: As I saw how closed I was, I began to open. If anything had become clear to me in the passing year, it was that any moment can be transforming, because it is the act of seeing itself that transforms. The kind of choiceless seeing that I had tried meant surrendering to each moment; it was a moment-by-moment letting go that suffused me with the energy and wider vision that seems to come when we face reality in a direct way. I knew that these moments of seeing would ac-cumulate to guide me, if only I remembered to try.

Still, I wanted to know more. I was intrigued by something that Sheikh Nur al Jerrahi had told us. "There is a principle of guidance in the universe," he had said. "We are being guided, moment by moment, in very subtle ways. It's there, a reservoir, a presence. But to become conscious of it—that is where the methods of the religious traditions are useful."

I wanted to know more about these methods. I wanted to learn what part the traditions, with their thousands of years of wisdom and method, could teach me about transformation. I especially wanted to know more about surrender and about the moment-by-moment effort to let go in order to open more, which Jeff and I had come to consider the very heart of our search.

That was why I was visiting the New York Buddhist Church. There, I would meet Taitetsu Unno, Jill Ker Conway Professor of Religion at Smith College, and an expert on Shin Buddhism. Shin, a form of Pure Land Buddhism founded in Japan in the thirteenth century, emphasizes surrendering "self-power" to the "Other-power" of Amida Buddha, a great cosmic buddha whose boundless compassion is a sacred energy that pervades all of life with "infinite light" and "infinite life."

The grey stone building on Riverside Drive that housed the church looked much like the surrounding buildings except for the ten-foot-high statue of Shinran, the founder of Shin, that stood in the courtyard appraising passersby with serene detachment. Inside, the building looked nothing like the austere *zendos* or exotic Tibetan centers that most Americans associate with Buddhism. It looked, in fact, like a church. The forty or so people who had gathered that day to hear Unno sat in folding metal chairs facing an elaborate, tiered altar. At lunchtime, we were served fruit salad and slices from a giant hero sandwich by nice Japanese-American women who cheerfully referred to their religion as "householder Buddhism" or "faith Buddhism." They knew that despite its long lineage in the States—it has been here for over a century—Shin, with its huge Asian following, hasn't attracted the many white, middle-class Americans that Zen and Tibetan Buddhism have. Shin doesn't offer meditation, so most Americans searching for a firsthand experience of enlightenment think it lacks spiritual promise and esoteric cachet.

Unno, a diminutive, kindly, sixtyish man who is also an expert on Zen, is used to Americans dismissing Shin as a kind of Sunday Buddhism because of its emphasis on faith over meditation. During lunch, as we balanced paper plates on our laps, I asked him about the role of surrender in Buddhist practice, and he tried to give me a sense of the profound awakening that an act of faith can bring.

"In the first place," he said, "surrender is a Western religious category. Objectively speaking, in Buddhism, surrender is at the core of giving up the ego self. But we don't use a special term for it because the whole of Buddhist life revolves around surrender, giving up the ego. There is a cultural problem here. I can use the example of the martial arts. In this country, martial arts are described as 'self-defense.' In the martial arts in East Asia—and I know something about the Japanese tradition, I've studied judo and aikido—the aim is to train to such an extent that there is no self to defend. That's very hard for Westerners to understand."

"How can we learn to surrender the ego self?" I asked.

"In this particular tradition of Shin Buddhism, it is taught that I can never surrender myself. Resistance comes from the deepest center of my karmic self. That's why the Buddha

Amida's compassion says, 'Tai, you don't have to surrender.' When I hear that, I understand that I can't do it because it's not in my nature to surrender; that's like asking me to fly to the sky. Then, naturally and spontaneously, the surrender takes place. As long as I think I can do it, it's not going to happen.

"In Shin, in the Pure Land tradition," Unno told me, "it comes down to listening to the teaching. There is no meditative practice as such. Listening *is* becoming awakened. I have my view of things and Buddhism presents its views. Gradually, my views are displaced by the views that Buddhism has cultivated for 2,500 years."

Unno commented further on the way that Americans try to "leapfrog to enlightenment."

"We were recently in Japan for six months," he said, "and while I was there I was reading articles and essays that Buddhist laypeople and monks wrote. One article was by the very distinguished abbot of a huge Zen monastery, who wrote, 'In Zen, there are only three things. First, cleaning. And second, chanting. And third, devotion. That's all.' Many Americans go to Zen hoping to get enlightened, but they don't want to do the cleaning. It's very demanding and rigorous. You get up at 3:00 A.M. and you not only sweep the floor but you have to mop it. On your knees, you know? And then you have to chant, for an hour in the morning, an hour at night. You can understand why a bright young American boy might say, 'What am I wasting my time for? I want to get enlightened.' But enlightenment cannot be separated from the daily chore of cleaning and sweeping and polishing—and the chanting and devotion."

Struck by Shin's emphasis on transferring "self-power" into "Other-power," I asked Unno if he saw a similarity between A.A. and Shin.

"I think there is an analogy there," he replied. "The first thing that A.A. stresses is admitting the powerlessness of the self, and no young, educated American wants to join a church that says that, first, you have to admit to powerlessness. I think that the contrast, however, is that in Shin and Pure Land compassion is at the base, not only in the sense that we try to be compassionate toward others but in the sense that we ourselves are the objects of compassion. We have received the compassion of Amida, and whatever I do is not what I do but is simply a movement that has come from Amida and is now going out. I am just a shell, an instrument of that compassion."

I wondered if I was imposing a Western interpretation on Shin. I asked Unno to describe how the faithful allowed surrender to happen.

"We use the expression 'returning home.' When we submit to something, we're not just giving up our egos, we're returning to the home of homes. The first poem I quoted this morning is from a Japanese haiku poem by Ryokan. He says, 'Return to Amida/return to Amida/so even dewdrops fall.' The dewdrops vanish. He's saying the things of this world are as fragile as dewdrops on a summer morning, so you must entrust yourself not to these things but to immeasurable life. Amida is immeasurable life. Everything in life, every event, is urging us to submit ourselves to immeasurable life."

Finally I asked Unno whether he thought that awakening could, as my experience showed, happen spontaneously, outside the context of a tradition.

"Yes," he answered, "but in order to enrich those kinds of experiences, you want to place it in a context, usually some religious context. Because I am a Shin Buddhist, I place experiences like that in the context of my particular tradition."

Ah, Lord! I worship Thee, the Undivided,
  The Uttermost of thought,
  The Treasure-Palace wrought
To hold the wealth of the worlds; the shield provided

  To shelter Virtue's laws;
  The Fount whence Life's stream draws
All waters of all rivers of all being:
  The One Unborn, Unending:
  Unchanging and unblending!
With might and majesty, past thought, past seeing![1]
                                   —BHAGAVAD GITA

A few weeks after I met with Taitetsu Unno, I spoke over the phone with Joseph Goldstein, a cofounder of the Insight Meditation Society in Barre, Massachusetts. As a teacher of Vipassana mediation, which emphasizes the examination of the nature of things through the act of seeing, Goldstein, I thought, could help me understand more about surrender in the moment.

"I visited a Pure Land church the other day," I told Goldstein, "and it was very interesting. There, emphasis is placed on trusting the wisdom that comes from Amida Buddha, without any meditative practice. Yet at the Insight Meditation Society, obviously meditation is emphasized. How do you see this?"

"I think the whole path," Goldstein answered, "all of its different aspects and forms, is comprised of skillful means. With different people at different times, different means are appropriate. I think sometimes the different traditions look very different from the outside because the forms are different, but that the actual qualities that are being cultivated by the various practices might look much more similar if viewed from the inside.

"I'm not very familiar with Pure Land schools," he added, "but I would imagine that part of what happens in their practice is that, through the vehicle of devotion or prayer, the mind begins to rest in undistracted awareness. In this aspect at least, in using the vehicle of devotion to open the mind to undistracted awareness, Pure Land is not so different from Vipassana. So what I find interesting in all the different schools is where all the different forms are leading. There are probably some great similarities in the actions that are being cultivated."

I wondered whether Goldstein thought this similarity applied to the very different practices and beliefs of Christians and Buddhists as well. Were a Christian at prayer and a Buddhist at meditation cultivating a similar state, and even similar perceptions?

"I think they might be. The particular belief system, or metaphysics, that overlays the practice may have profound consequences, however. Even though the practices of different traditions are leading to openness, compassion, love, and awareness, depending on the particular teaching, the same understanding isn't necessarily going to come. Experiences depend on the conceptual framework in which they occur. We can appreciate the similarities even while recognizing that there might be differences in understanding.

"One of the aspects of surrender that probably comes from many traditions and that is very much a part of the meditative process," he pointed out, "is an attitude of openness to the unknown. Surrender is important because otherwise we remain limited by our level of understanding—and unless you're a supremely omniscient Buddha, your understanding is going to be limited."

I asked Goldstein to comment a bit more about the relationship of meditation to the process of letting go and opening up to the unknown.

"We talk a lot about surrender in each moment—being open to what's around you, choosing without preference. There's a nice phrase from the Taoist tradition that says, 'to be open to the ten thousand joys and the ten thousand sorrows.' That quality of willingness to experience the full range of the human condition without our usual conditions of accepting what's pleasant and rejecting what's unpleasant—that's surrender in the meditative practice, which also carries over into our lives. To experience fully whatever is around you."

"If I want to understand surrender," I followed up, "is this where I begin? In small ways, from moment to moment?"

"I think we can begin on any level," Goldstein replied. "For example, the act of taking refuge [the first formal step in Buddhism, which includes 'taking refuge' in the Buddha, in the dharma, or teaching, and in the *sangha*] is really an act of surrender, of opening up, of acknowledging something larger. By something larger I don't necessarily mean a supernatural being but, rather, the possibility of the awakening mind. To take refuge in the Buddha or the *sangha* is an acknowledgment of something bigger than our egocentric selves."

And God spake unto Noah, and to his sons with him, saying,

And I, behold, I establish my covenant with you, and with your seed after you;

And with every living creature that *is* with you, of the fowl, of the cattle, and of every beast of the earth from all that go out of the ark, to every beast of the earth.

> And I will establish my covenant with you; neither
> shall all flesh be cut off any more by the waters of a flood;
> neither shall there any more be a flood to destroy the
> earth.
>
> And God said, This is the token of the covenant which I
> make between me and you and every living creature that *is*
> with you, for perpetual generations....
>
> —GENESIS 9:8–12

Taitetsu Unno and Joseph Goldstein offered valuable insight through their understandings of two different yet complementary Buddhist traditions. I wanted to know more about the part surrender plays in the Judaeo-Christian tradition, however, and about what it might mean to surrender to the guidance of a religious tradition. For this, I turned to my sister-in-law, Carol Zaleski, who spoke with me by phone from her home in Northampton.

My conversation with Carol began with my telling her about my recent talks with Unno and Goldstein. "To Goldstein," I explained, "surrender seems almost synonymous with seeing in the moment, with letting go of things as they arise during the act of sitting meditation. But in the Pure Land Church, as I understand it, surrender involves a complete abandonment of yourself to an Other-power." I told Carol that I wanted to comprehend the relationship between these two understandings of surrender.

"A couple of years ago," she said. "I attended a conference on Buddhist-Christian dialogue. There were quite a few Zen people there, including an American Zen nun living in Japan. In a talk she gave about people who combine Buddhist and Christian practice, she spoke of her Zen training in a Rinzai monastery in Japan—an extremely rigorous training during which she suffered immensely, physically and psychologically and spiritually. I sensed that her experience was entirely about surrender, and this without her being involved in any of the traditions that we think of as devotional."

For this nun, Carol explained, surrender involved a total acceptance of her experience of koan study and of sitting. "It seemed that, essentially, this nun would not have survived if she hadn't surrendered herself to the experience. Listening to her, it struck me that there's not such a great disparity between at least some kinds of Zen and what we associate with Pure Land Buddhism. They're both transformative paths, and whatever path you're on there's always a point when you realize that you can't get to the next step in the path by your own efforts. You have to surrender."

"What *is* surrender?" I asked.

"My own opinion is that surrender is the specifically religious element in every religion. Otherwise, what you have is morality, moral struggle. It's when morality passes over into surrender that you pass over from morality to religion."

And what gives surrender its religious character?

"As the A.A. people say," Carol answered, "you get in touch with a higher power. You realize that your own sources are inadequate and you allow yourself to be influenced by that other power. So there's an act of trust, of faith, a breaking down of the narrow ego self. And that doesn't occur by systematic technique, even if sometimes techniques are used. So there's always that moment of surrender. I know of no religion where this doesn't exist. And where it does exist, I immediately see religion at work."

Carol's words reminded me of a remark that Sheikh Nur al Jerrahi had made: that today, in America, there's an enormous faith in, and even greediness for, personal experience—and yet there is something that transcends experience. I asked her about this.

"The reason that we place so much stock in experience, excessive stock," she said, "is that in many people's minds other sources of information that are placed in the universe have been discredited—that is, tradition, authority, revelation. If we feel that we can't reliably consult those sources, we fall back on our own private experiences. And though experiential confirmation has always been considered important, and though no religious tradition has taught people that they should disregard their experience, the traditions do discipline experience and give it a language and a form, thereby making possible further experiences that otherwise would not have been possible."

This comment touched upon my own recent thoughts about the difference between submission and surrender. In some ways, I had been thinking, we may feel an innate longing for submission, and it may be this longing that can lead people to submit to an abusive spiritual teacher. But was this longing a purely neurotic impulse, or was it perhaps some vestigial form of a higher surrender that, in its original form, is characterized more by an impulse to higher service?

"I think all those impulses of submission, in the way you mean them," Carol said, "are distortions of higher impulses. Using the two terms helps to indicate the two parts of the spectrum. Of course, a problem arises in that *submission* is a translation for Islam. In Islam, though, what is meant is not submission to some petty tyrant who lords it over you, but submission to the one and only God, the same God who gives us our freedom. So our freedom and our obedience are completely intertwined. There's a kind of freedom that comes from obedience. You are freed because you are no longer acting out of your own selfish aims and fears. But that obedience works only with the absolute, with the transcendent. Whenever it's transferred to some imitator of that role, danger arises."

I asked Carol whether she could offer any final insight into surrender, transforming moments, and religion.

"I've been thinking about quoting William James to you." she said. "James divided the world into two kinds of religious temperaments—the healthy minded and what he called the 'sick soul.' Healthy minded people are those who naturally feel in harmony with the universe and who therefore don't need to go through a dramatic experience of surrender, because they are already attuned to things and don't have a strong sense of moral or spiritual discord or discrepancy. That's the attitude that James associated with what he called 'the mind-cure movement,' which is so pervasive today in the form of the New Age. But James thought this attitude was superficial because it didn't acknowledge evil.

"For someone," she added, "who has what James calls the sick soul, or the 'divided self'—someone who has a low threshold for noticing discord and evil and suffering in the world—the only way to achieve a sense of harmony or integration is to pass through surrender or a kind of death and then emerge with a higher kind of integration. That's what James called the 'conversion experience.' He thought the kind of religious attitude that comes from having been a sick soul and having gone through a conversion experience is more profound. And he said that Buddhism and Christianity, since they are both religions of deliverance, exhibit this pattern of death and rebirth, of conversion—of passing through surrender and then integration. As a result, he considered them much more profound than any of the newer, eclectic spiritualities that have continued to this day under the guise of the New Age."

Perhaps the most famous conversion experience is that of Saul of Tarsus, who is better known as St. Paul, on the road to Damascus. Before his conversion, Saul was a persecutor of the earliest Christians "unto the death, binding and delivering into prisons both men and women," as he admits in the Acts of the Apostles, 22:4. He was traveling to Damascus to bring back Christian prisoners from that city to Jerusalem when:

> ...it came to pass, that, as I made my journey, and was come nigh unto Damascus about noon, suddenly there shone from heaven a great light around me.
>
> And I fell unto the ground, and heard a voice saying to me, Saul, Saul, why persecutest thou me?
>
> And I answered, Who are thou, Lord? And he said unto me, I am Jesus of Nazareth, whom thou persecutest.
>
> And they that were with me saw indeed the light, and were afraid; but they heard not the voice of him that spake to me.
>
> And I said, What shall I do, Lord? And the Lord said unto me, Arise, and go into Damascus; and there it shall be told thee of all things which are appointed for thee to do.
>
> —ACTS 22:6–10

Conversion often consists of an accumulation of moments of awakening that lead up to as a definitive event that seals a new understanding. Saul's illumination occurred when the light shone upon him and he heard Jesus speak; in this moment, he surrendered himself to God and died to his old self. Yet Saul was probably already prepared—perhaps cultivated by the teachings he had been exposed to as a persecutor of Christians. And he needed to make the further step of integration—to take in the truth and make it his own—to complete his conversion. The light that shone down upon Saul blinded him ("I could not see for the glory of the light"). In order to see again, he needed to go to Damascus and there speak with a disciple named Ananias:

> And Ananias went his way, and entered into the house; and putting his hands on him said, Brother Saul, the Lord, *even* Jesus, that appeared unto thee in the way as thou camest, hath sent me, that thou mightest receive thy sight, and be filled with the Holy Ghost.
>
> And immediately there fell from his eyes as it had been scales: and he received sight forthwith, and arose, and was baptized.
>
> —ACTS 9:17–18

Each moment in which we try to see ourselves as we are, we engage in a process of conversion to our true nature. In flashes we may see that what we really are is a witnessing attention, an open reality that can embrace both self and Self. Awakening to this reality can become part of our everyday life; yet, like Saul, we may need the help of others to make it our own. The traditions are our Ananias: They possess methods and wisdom that can help us to see.

"By your fruits ye shall know them," Jesus said. It is perhaps by the fruits of the religious traditions—by the men and women through whom they unfold—that we have known the traditions best. Two experiences Tracy and I have had in recent years with a leader of a tradition have shown me something about what the great religions have to offer. Both experiences involve a Buddhist, the Dalai Lama; but what we saw in him, I am convinced, is manifest in representatives of each of the traditions.

The first encounter took place in 1990, shortly after the Dalai Lama had been awarded the Nobel Prize for Peace. With Tracy, I attended a press conference that the Tibetan leader gave at a midtown Manhattan hotel. After taking questions, the Dalai Lama walked through the throng of reporters and journalists, many of whom, myself included, crowded around him trying to shake his hand. At the time, tensions between China and Tibet were at a peak, so a phalanx of handlers walked alongside the new Nobel laureate for protection, directing his movement as he made his way through the exit door. When these men shepherded him by me right after he had shaken Tracy's hand, I felt a pang of disappointment.

To my surprise, after greeting some people with his back to me, the Dalai Lama turned around and stepped toward me. He reached down, clasped my hands in both of his, and bowed. It was clear to me that he had noted my distress and, despite the press of time and his handlers, had acted to relieve it. It was a small gesture, but coming from a world leader who could just as easily have ignored me, one that moved me.

In October of the following year, over the course of three days, Tracy and I witnessed the Dalai Lama give the Kalachakra initiation—an ancient Tantric ritual of empowerment attributed to the Buddha—at New York City's Paramount Theater. During these three days, the Paramount stage, one of the city's largest, looked like a vision from another world. Hundreds of Tibetan monks in red and yellow robes sat or kneeled shoulder to shoulder at stage right. Above them hung three giant *thangkas* depicting the universe as a whirl of energy and form, while at stage left stood a huge silk tent representing a divine palace. The audience of nearly three thousand was just as colorful, a mix of intellectuals clad in Manhattan black, Tibetan refugees holding offerings of food and flowers, scholars, hippies, celebrities, and pilgrims.

At center stage stood a high throne. There, the Dalai Lama, monarch to the monks and considered by them to be a living god, would take on the attributes of the deity Kalachakra in order to transmit a sacred wisdom.

We first became aware that the Dalai Lama had stepped onto the stage when the mass of monks began to stir; noticing the commotion, the audience turned their heads toward stage right. There, a moment later, we spotted the Tibetan leader making his way through the excited monks. He moved slowly because as each monk greeted him, he stopped and bowed, his hands templed in prayer. When he finally reached the throne, he lowered himself to the ground and prostrated.

That the Dalai Lama had stopped to bow to nearly every monk astonished me. It reminded me of how Jesus washed the feet of his disciples. Later, I realized that by shaking my hand at the press conference, and by bowing to me and to his monks and subjects, the Dalai Lama may have been honoring the sacred in each of us, and in himself. This attention, it seemed, was a demonstration of how someone guided by a tradition can express through himself and his actions the fundamental truth taught by every tradition: that we are each connected to the divine.

A PARTING THOUGHT

FOR A LONG TIME AFTER I SAW THE LIGHT, I FELT BEREFT, as if a wonderful guest had come and gone, leaving a palpable sense of absence. I thought I would never see that guest again and I haven't, at least not in such a definite way. But over the years, I have come to respect that absence as a kind of invisible presence that reminds me of what is possible.

These days my spiritual search, like my creative efforts, is very much about accepting my limits and embracing my own experience. I now know that I can't make anything happen—I can't force a dramatic encounter with the divine. But in rare moments when I abandon all ambition and resolve simply to see what is, that accepting attention works a subtle kind of magic. When I fully accept myself and what is around me, I can begin to sense the presence of what is hidden. Now I know that there are depths in reality, unseen connections and meanings. As I learn to open to it moment by moment, impression by impression, it might lead me back to the light.

Therefore I am my own first cause, both of my eternal being and of my temporal being. To this end I was born, and by virtue of my birth being eternal, I shall never die. It is of the nature of this eternal birth that I have been eternally, that I am now, and shall be forever. What I am as a temporal creature is to die and come to nothingness, for it came within time, and so with time it will pass away. In my eternal birth, however, everything was begotten. I was my own first cause, as well as the cause of everything else. If I had willed it, neither I nor the world would have come to be! If I had not been, there would have been no god. There is, however, no need to understand this.[1]

—MEISTER ECKHART

TRANSFORMING
MOMENTS

A transforming moment may be as subtle as an awareness of the breath or as dramatic as an encounter with God. Here are several first-person accounts of awakenings, ancient and modern, Eastern and Western, that indicate the range of ways in which an opening to the sacred may come:

CLAIRE BOOTH LUCE LEFT HER MARK ON THIS CENTURY AS a journalist, playwright, congresswoman, and ambassador to Italy. During her adolescence, she experienced this resonant moment of spiritual awakening, as described in *The Road to Damascus: The Spiritual Pilgrimage of Fifteen Converts to Catholicism*:

It is an experience which occurred when I was perhaps sixteen or seventeen years old. I no longer remember where it took place, except that it was a summer day on an American beach....

I remember that it was a cool, clean, fresh, calm, blue, radiant day, and that I stood by the shore, my feet not in the waves. And now—as then—I find it difficult to explain what did happen. I expect that the easiest thing to say is that suddenly SOMETHING WAS. My whole soul was cleft clean by it, as a silk veil slit by a shining sword. And I *knew*. I do not know now what I knew. I remember, I didn't know even then. That is, I didn't *know* with any "faculty." It was not in my mind or heart or blood stream. But whatever it was I knew, it was something that made ENORMOUS SENSE. And it was final. And yet that word could not be used, for it meant end, and there was no end to this finality. Then joy abounded in all of me. Or rather, I abounded in joy. I seemed to have no nature, and yet my whole nature was adrift in this immense joy, as a speck of dust is seen to dance in a great golden shaft of sunlight.

I don't know how long this experience lasted. It was, I should think, closer to a second than an hour—though it might have been either. . . .[1]

◆

One of the most influential of all transforming moments occurred in 1934, in a detox hospital in New York City. There, drunkard Bill Wilson, cofounder of A.A., lying in bed in the midst of another grueling treatment for yet another binge, had an experience that helped show him the way to freedom from alcohol:

My depression deepened unbearably and finally it seemed to me as though I were at the bottom of the pit. I still gagged badly on the notion of a Power greater than myself, but finally, just for the moment, the last vestige of my proud obstinacy was crushed. All at once I found my crying out, "If there is a God, let Him show Himself! I am ready to do anything, anything!"

Suddenly the room lit up with a great white light. I was caught up into an ecstasy which there are no words to describe. It seemed to me, in the mind's eye, that I was on a mountain and that a wind not of air but of spirit was blowing. And then it burst upon me that I was a free man. Slowly the ecstasy subsided. I lay on the bed, but now for a time I was in another world, a new world of consciousness. All about me and through me there was a wonderful feeling of Presence, and I thought to myself, "So this is the God of preachers!"[2]

◆

In 1988, David Chadwick, a veteran American Zen monk, flew to Japan to study at a Japanese Zen monastery, an experience he describes with humor and insight in his book *Thank You and OK!: An American Zen Failure in Japan*. This brief excerpt details a moment of awareness that came to Chadwick during a sitting meditation:

One morning sitting zazen and waiting my turn for sanzen, I saw Mind, not as obscure or deep or hidden, but as superficial and immediately available. I sat there breathing and before long I was thinking about how to get our new video camera working. Then I moved on to the day's schedule. I caught myself and wondered how much of a hindrance these thoughts were. The pulling power of my thinking was low and an image arose with the phrase "bones in the corner of the cage." Yep, just old meatless bones I'm gnawing on. And then I thought, well what am I then, the cage? I experienced myself as that room with the cement walls and metal bars, the floor with the bones on it, and some water in a trough by the edge. Hm. The cage? Is that it? I sat and watched and then from within I heard breathing and sensed movement and saw a lion's tail sweep around before me in a circular path.[3]

◆

Presbyterian minister Charles G. Finney served as president of Oberlin College from 1851 to 1866. At age twenty-nine, thirty years before he began his tenure at Oberlin, he was granted an extraordinary transformative experience after moving some furniture and books to a new office with a colleague:

> By evening we got the books and furniture adjusted; and I made up, in an open fireplace, a good fire, hoping to spend the evening alone. Just as dark Squire—seeing that everything was adjusted, bade me goodnight and went to his home. I had accompanied him to the door; and as I closed the door and turned around, my heart seemed to be liquid within me. All my feelings seemed to rise and flow out; and the utterance of my heart was, "I want to pour my whole soul out to God." The rising of my soul was so great that I rushed into the room back of the front office, to pray.
>
> There was no fire, and no light, in the room; nevertheless it appeared to me as if it were perfectly light. As I went in and shut the door after me, it seemed as if I met the Lord Jesus Christ face to face. It did not occur to me then, nor did it for some time afterward, that it was a wholly mental state. On the contrary it seemed to me that I saw him as I would see any other man. He said nothing, but looked at me in such a manner as to break me right down at his feet. I have always since regarded this as a most remarkable state of mind; for it seemed to me a reality, that he stood before me, and I fell down at his feet and poured out my soul to him. I wept aloud like a child, and made such confessions as I could

with my choked utterance. It seemed to me that I bathed his feet with my tears; and yet I had no distinct impression that I touched him, that I recollect.

I must have continued in this state for a good while; but my mind was too absorbed with the interview to recollect anything that I said. But I know, as soon as my mind became calm enough to break off from the interview, I returned to the front office, and found that the fire that I had made of large wood was nearly burned out. But as I turned and was about to take a seat by the fire, I received a mighty baptism of the Holy Ghost. Without any expectation of it, without ever having the thought in my mind that there was any such thing for me, without any recollection that I had ever heard the thing mentioned by any person in the world, the Holy Spirit descended upon me in a manner that seemed to go through me, body and soul. I could feel the impression, like a wave of electricity, going through and through me. Indeed it seemed to have come in waves and waves of liquid love; for I could not express it in any other way. It seemed like the very breath of God. I can recollect distinctly that it seemed to fan me, like immense wings.

No words can express the wonderful love that was shed abroad in my heart. I wept aloud with joy and love; and I do not know but I should say, I literally bellowed out the unutterable gushings of my heart. These waves came over me, and over me, and over me, one after the other, until I recollect I cried out, "I shall die if these waves continue to pass over me." I said, "Lord, I cannot bear any more"; yet I had no fear of death.

How long I continued in this state, with this baptism continuing to roll over me and go through me, I do not know. But I know it was late in the evening when a member of my choir—for I was the leader of the choir—came into my office to see me. He was a member of the church. He found me in this state of loud weeping, and said to me, "Mr. Finney, what ails you?" I could make him no answer for some time. He then said, "Are you in pain?" I gathered myself up as best I could, and replied, "No, but so happy that I cannot live."[4]

From William Wordsworth's *The Prelude; or Growth of a Poet's Mind:*

> *That awful Power rose from the mind's abyss*
> *Like an unfathomed vapour that enwraps,*
> *At once, some lonely traveller. I was lost;*
> *Halted without an effort to break through;*
> *But to my conscious soul I now can say—*
> *"I recognize the glory"; in such strength*
> *Of usurpation, when the light of sense*
> *Goes out, but with a flash that has revealed*
> *The invisible world, doth greatness make abode.*

Rachel Cowan, a New Englander whose ancestors arrived on the *Mayflower,* converted from Episcopalianism to Judaism after marrying Paul Cowan. In an interview for *The God I Believe In,* she describes a moment of awakening that came to her shortly after her husband's death:

Like Buber, I would say this is real, these very intense I-thou moments which are very, very brief and quite far be-

163

tween. I was walking with Isa on a vacation we took together the year Paul died. We went to the state of Washington, to some lake in the middle of the wilderness. We got off
the boat and I looked up at these mountains and I said to
myself, "Paul, where are you? These mountains are cold; they
are stone; this earth is stone; we are just these little bits of
flesh passing by. What is the point of all this and what
happened to you?" I started to cry. It just seemed so over-
whelmingly bleak. Then the next morning, I was out walking and all of a sudden I absolutely knew that Paul was with
me and I absolutely knew that he was part of God. His presence was real, but it was a presence that was linked to the
presence of God. Nobody said anything, but I felt incredible
relief and comfort. When I am feeling really lonely, really sad
and depressed, the memory of that experience gives me
strength to go on.[5]

◆

Paul Brunton (1898–1981) devoted his life to gaining
firsthand knowledge of spiritual wisdom both Eastern and
Western and relaying his understandings through a series of
influential books. Here, from his son's moving memoir of
him, *Paul Brunton: A Personal View,* by Kenneth Thurston
Hurst, is a passage drawn from Brunton's own description of
the "illumination" that came upon him after years of study
and practice:

> Suddenly, I realized that this was a crushing of the self by an
> unknown power beyond myself. It was then that I began fer-
> vently to pray, feeling forlorn, humbled, terrified and lost. I
> lost the feeling of the passage of time. I felt severed from

earthly reality and became dizzy at the thought that I had reached the end of my endurance. Then I swooned. The moments just before I fainted were filled with indescribable horror. But I soon awoke. A tiny flame of hope appeared in my heart. And then it grew and grew. My first thought was that God was answering my prayers. I began gradually to feel close to the people around me once more; closer than ever before. Some hours later reassurance gradually returned to me and I felt mature and newly born. Enlightenment seemed to come.

Next a feeling of oneness with God followed. I seemed to know and understand much that I had never understood before. My ego was going and my happiness increased every moment. I felt that this newfound faith would guide me through every possible situation....

The Divine Presence seemed to be very near. In fact, I knew that it was in my real essence. Whenever any difficulties or problems arose, I found that all I had to do to solve them was to say, "Not my will but Thy will be done."[6]

◆

C. S. Lewis (1898–1963), author of *The Screwtape Letters* and *The Narnia Chronicles,* was a proud young atheist professor when, as described in his book *Surprised by Joy,* he surrendered to the divine:

Remember, I had always wanted, above all things, not to be "interfered with." I had wanted (mad wish) "to call my soul my own." I had been far more anxious to avoid suffering than to achieve delight. I had always aimed at limited liabilities. The supernatural itself had been to me, first, an illicit dram, and then, as by a drunkard's reaction, nauseous.... I had pretty well known that my idea of virtue would never be allowed to lead me into anything tolerably painful; I would be "reasonable." But now what had been an ideal became a command; and what might not be expected of one? Doubtless, by definition, God was Reason itself. But would He also be "reasonable" in that other, more comfortable sense? Not the slightest assurance on that score was offered me. Total surrender, the absolute leap in the dark, were demanded. The reality with which no treaty can be made was upon me. . . .

You must picture me alone in that room in Magdalen, night after night, feeling, whenever my mind lifted even for a second from my work, the steady, unrelenting approach of Him whom I so earnestly desired not to meet. That which I greatly feared had at last come upon me. In the Trinity Term of 1929 I gave in, and admitted that God was God, and knelt and prayed; perhaps that night, the most dejected and reluctant convert in all of England.[7]

————◆————

In 1989, Gavin Harrison, a teacher of insight meditation, was diagnosed as HIV+. His book *In the Lap of the Buddha* offers a compassionate account of his life and how he has come to grips with his illness. In the following excerpt, he tells how, during a climb of the volcano Haleakala on the Hawaiian island of Maui, he experienced the sort of fleeting transforming moment that we all have, a moment in which, as he puts it, "we touch a deeper truth and feel fully alive":

Full of feelings of being both near and far away from home, I decided to hike down into the crater. Haleakala is dormant, of course. The trail leads two thousand feet down through an alien domain of magnificent black, red, and gray lava rock, dotted with the huge cinder cones that spewed out lava in prehistoric times. The only plant that can live inside the crater is the silver sword, an endangered species that looks a little like yucca, but without a spike. . . .

I was alone. It was deadly quiet. I sat down on a piece of lava rock and looked out on the cinder cones that rose up from the floor of the crater. I was transfixed by the spectacle around me. For a moment my mind grappled and struggled to find some sort of reference for what I was seeing. There immediately rose a deep sense of knowing that this place was simply beyond comparison. There were no references. For the longest time, I sat there, awed, like a child. Nothing stirred, either within or outside of me.

In letting go of the absurdity and even the arrogance of believing that we know what the next moment will bring, we relinquish our grip on reality and surrender into the mystery of not knowing, moment to moment, what will appear next in awareness.[8]

◆

From Walt Whitman's *Song of Myself,* in *Leaves of Grass:*

I believe in you, my soul, the other I am must not abase
*   itself to you,*
And you must not be abased to the other.

Loafe with me on the grass, loose the stop from your throat,
Not words, not music or rhyme I want, not custom or
*   lecture, not even the best,*
Only the lull I like, the hum of your valved voice.

I mind how once we lay such a transparent summer morning,
How you settled your head athwart my hips and gently turn'd
over upon me,
And parted the shirt from my bosom-bone, and plunged
your tongue to my bare-stript heart,
And reach'd till you felt my beard, and reach'd till you held
my feet.

Swiftly arose and spread around me the peace and knowledge
that pass all the arguments of the earth,
And I know that the hand of God is the promise of my own,
And I know that the spirit of God is the brother of my own,
And that all the men ever born are also my brothers, and the
women my sisters and lovers,
And that a kelson of the creation is love.

◆

A moment of awakening can instill terror rather than enlightenment if the recipient isn't prepared for it. As described
in this passage from Christopher Isherwood's *The Wishing
Tree,* when Vivekananda, who was to spread Hindu teachings
throughout the United States, first met his teacher, the great
Indian saint Ramakrishna, he was granted a vision more
powerful than he could bear:

> Muttering something to himself, with his eyes fixed on
> me, he [Ramakrishna] slowly drew near me ... In the twin-
> kling of an eye, he placed his right foot on my body. At his
> touch, I had an entirely new experience. With my eyes wide
> open, I saw that the walls and everything else in the room
> were whirling around, vanishing into nothingness; the

whole universe, together with my own individuality, was about to be lost in an all-encompassing, mysterious Void! I was terribly frightened and thought I must be facing death—for the loss of my individuality meant nothing less than that to me. I couldn't control myself: I cried out, "What are you doing to me! I have my parents at home!" At this, he laughed aloud. Stroking my chest, he said, "All right, that's enough for now. Everything will come in time." The wonderful thing was, as soon as he'd said that, the whole experience came to an end. I was myself again. And everything inside and outside the room was just as it had been before.[9]

◆

In his book *Open Mind, Discriminating Mind: Reflections on Human Possibilities,* psychologist Charles Tart offers a rare glimpse into the meditating mind by describing his moment-to-moment experience as he tries to awaken while recording the effort on his word processor:

So now the particular form of mindfulness meditation I usually practice begins. My goal is to be completely attentive to whatever physical sensations come along. As a sensation arises in my body I will pay attention to it. . . .

I close my eyes. My attention broadens out from my abdomen, where it was focused in concentrative meditation, moving out to encompass my whole body. I notice a tightness in my head that I wasn't aware of a moment before, but which feels like a familiar tension pattern. Some of it is jaw and temple tightness, which partly relaxes as I perceive it more fully.

I recall that I'm focusing on what's happening in my body in order to relax it or make it feel better. I'm just focusing on whatever is there. If it relaxes and feels better, that's fine. If it doesn't relax, that's also fine. My goal is to sense it completely and follow whatever happens by itself, not control it.

My find fills with a sensation of "vibration" through my whole body. "Vibration" seems a grandiose sort of word, maybe tingling would be better. My intellectual mind cuts in: "Is this an *important* feeling? A *useful* sensation?" Realizing I'm not here to *think about* my sensations in this meditation, I let the thought go. Fortunately, I feel, it goes readily, without generating more thoughts. . . .[10]

In his *Confessions* (A.D. 400), St. Augustine, "Doctor of the Church," repents of his profligate youth and his embrace of the dualistic philosophy of Manichaeism. In the following passage, he describes the awakening that brought him to Christianity at age thirty-two:

> But when a deep consideration had from the secret bottom of my soul drawn together and heaped up all my misery in the sight of my heart; there arose a mighty storm, bringing a mighty shower of tears. Which that I might pour forth wholly, in its natural expressions, I rose from Alypius: solitude was suggested to me as fitter for the business of weeping; so I retired so far that even his presence could not be a burden to me. Thus was it then with me, and he perceived something of it; for something I suppose I had spoken, wherein the tones of my voice appeared choked with weeping, and so had risen up. He then remained where we were sitting, most extremely astonished. I cast myself down

I know not how, under a certain fig-tree, giving full vent to my tears; and the floods of mine eyes gushed out, an *acceptable sacrifice to Thee.* And, not indeed in these words, yet to this purpose, spake I much unto Thee: *And Thou, O Lord, how long? how long, Lord, wilt Thou be angry, for ever? Remember not our former inequities,* for I felt that I was held by them. I sent up these sorrowful words: *How long? how long, "to-morrow, and to-morrow?" Why not now? why not is there this hour an end to my uncleanliness?*

So was I speaking, and weeping in the most bitter contrition of my heart, when lo! I heard from a neighboring house a voice, as of boy or girl, I know not, chanting, and oft repeating, "Take up and read; Take up and read." Instantly my countenance altered, I began to think most intently, whether children were wont in any kind of play to sing such words; nor could I remember ever to have heard the like. So checking the torrent of my tears, I arose; interpreting it to be no other than a command from God, to open the book, and read the first chapter I should find. For I had heard of Antony, that coming in during the reading of the Gospel, he received the admonition, as if what was being read, was spoken to him; *Go sell all that thou hast, and give it to the poor, and thou shalt have treasure in heaven, and come and follow me.* And by such oracle he was forthwith converted unto Thee. Eagerly then I returned to the place where Alypius was sitting; for there had I laid the volume of the Apostle, when I arose thence. I seized, opened, and in silence read that section, on which my eyes first fell: *Not in rioting and drunkenness, not in chambering and wantonness, not in strife and envying; but put ye on the Lord Jesus Christ, and make not provision for the flesh,* in concupiscence. No further would I read; nor needed I; for instantly at the end of this sentence, by a light as it were of serenity infused into my heart, all the darkness of doubt vanished away.[11]

———◆———

Participation in a sacred rite can lead to a moment of transformation. Here, as reported in Rabbi Daniel B. Syme's *Why I Am a Reform Jew,* is what came to Caitlin O'Sullivan, born and raised Catholic, during an early exploration of Judaism:

> One Friday evening, I decided I wanted to light Shabbat candles. I asked my friend if it was all right—was there anything wrong with it if I wasn't Jewish? He assured me that lightning would not strike me, nor an earthquake swallow me up. He helped me learn the blessing and we talked about the various customs involved in the physical act of kindling the light. I picked something that seemed to work with my personality and I did it. As I opened my eyes and beheld the light I had created, I was moved as I had never been moved in my life. In that moment, I understood the concept of mystery, of spirit, of invoking a power greater than myself, through myself. I understand that by activating something very deep and personal, I could also touch something as incomprehensible as the light of the stars in the universe. In that moment, I was changed forever, utterly changed.[12]

———◆———

Until she was six years old, Helen Keller was a bitter child, exiled from the world by blindness and deafness. In late 1877, through the patient instruction of her teacher, Anne Sullivan, she was in one glorious moment released from her psychic prison:

We walked down the path to the well-house, attracted by the fragrance of the honeysuckle with which it was covered. Some one was drawing water and my teacher placed my hand under the spout. As the cool stream gushed over one hand she spelled into the other the word *water*, at first slowly, then rapidly. I stood still, my whole attention fixed upon the motion of her fingers. Suddenly I felt a misty consciousness as of something forgotten—a thrill of returning thought; and somehow the mystery of language was revealed to me. I knew then that "w-a-t-e-r" meant the wonderful cool something that was flowing over my hand. That living word awakened my soul, gave it light, hope, joy, set it free! There were barriers still, it is true, but barriers that could in time be swept away.

I learned a great many new words that day. I do not remember what they all were; but I do know that *mother, father, sister, teacher* were among them—words that were to make the world blossom for me, "like Aaron's rod, with flowers." It would have been difficult to find a happier child than I was as I lay in my crib at the close of that eventful day and lived over the joys it had brought me, and for the first time longed for a new day to come.[13]

◆

From Lord Alfred Tennyson's *Ancient Sage:*

More than once when I
Sat all alone, revolving in myself
The word that is the symbol of myself,

The mortal limit of the Self was loosed,
And passed into the nameless, as a cloud
Melts into heaven. I touch'd my limbs, the limbs
Were strange, not mine—and yet no shade of doubt,
But utter clearness, and thro' loss of Self
The gain of such large life as matched with ours
Were sun to spark—unshadowable in words,
Themselves but shadows of a shadow-world.

———◆———

The following is the transcription, slightly edited, of a tape-recorded account of an encounter with the sacred experienced by a friend of ours, Larry Swimmer, many years ago:

I was in my early twenties when this occurred. It was a time of great seeking for me, and of great suffering. I was with a group of friends. We were all seekers together, seeking the light with great zeal. One day we went for a hike in the woods around Woodstock, where one of the fellows, a meditator, lived. He took us to a very unusual place. It was a dried-up waterfall, with lots of outcroppings of rock that you could navigate and sit on. The rock had very unusual formations because it used to be washed by water.

We each went off on our own and sat, meditating. I don't know how much time passed but suddenly something started to happen to me. I started to go down a dark tunnel. I was traveling down the tunnel toward a light, a brilliant blue light. I remember that as I traveled toward the light, I felt tranquility. I remember feeling interest and I remember feeling a sense of knowing. At a certain point, I reached a place in this light. I don't know how to describe it—I was with the light.

At that point, my intellect was activated. This experience

174

is indescribable, really. It was nondimensional and not explainable in terms that we know. Everything I'm going to tell you is an attempt to explain with words a dimension of awareness that is not of this world. Nor was this light from this world, in that it wasn't really a light. It seemed like a light, but it was more than a light. It was almost like a view into a new dimension, another dimension.

I was aware that I was having a major spiritual experience. I remember realizing that this was a confirmation that life is a spiritual journey. This is what I had been waiting for. I had been asking questions, reading books, searching for answers, but nothing substantial had yet come to me from my own personal experience.

I was being transported, I was comforted, I was safe. I felt completely loved, accepted, cared for. The safety was greater than human safety. It was divine safety, complete safety. It preempted everything. It was total acceptance, a feeling of being home.

I don't remember much else about the experience except that I asked a question. I asked, "Well, what should I do about this now? Help me out, tell me what to do." And the answer I kept getting was, "It doesn't matter." This perplexed me for years and years, until recently I got it. I'll tell you about that in a minute.

I returned after some amount of time, it could have been a split second, it could have been an hour, I don't know. I returned to ordinary consciousness, with one exception: Still within my awareness was this blue light burning above me. It was a large glow, a brilliant, almost cobalt blue otherworldly light with a little white edging. And it continued on for days and days. Of course, I was totally shocked and didn't know what to make of this. It wasn't my imagination and it wasn't going away.

Gradually, it got smaller and receded. But it has never gone away. This light experience occurs to me very frequently, and has so for over twenty years now. It changes sizes. Sometimes it's a little flicker. Sometimes it's there for a long time, sometimes it's *not* there for a really long time, sometimes it's around frequently. I have no control over it. When I'm really agitated and in my darkest places, it usually doesn't appear. When I'm happy and joyful and light, it tends to appear. It has always served as a source of serenity for me, a little reminder that I'm loved and helped and cared for. And it's real, no matter what my ego may tell me at any given moment about what reality is.

Regarding the answer, "It doesn't matter," recently I realized that what really matters is God. We think all these things matter, that we have these important things to do. But we have nothing to do, really, but be connected to God. That's the only thing that matters.

◆

On Christmas Day 1978, Andrew Harvey, the youngest fellow ever elected to Oxford and critically acclaimed author of *A Journey to Ladakh,* had an encounter that was to transform his life. On that day, as he describes in his extraordinary book *Hidden Journey: A Spiritual Awakening,* he met the spiritual teacher known as Mother Meera, who was then seventeen. The first passage below gives Harvey's initial impression of Mother Meera; the second conveys how, months later, her presence had altered his perception of reality:

Meera sat quietly in the chair gazing down at her hands folded in her lap. One by one, in silence, the people in the room went up to kneel to her and let her take their heads between her hands and then look into her eyes. The silence she brought with her into the room was unlike any I had ever experienced—deeper, full of uncanny, wounding joy. . . . She did not take the worship offered for herself. There was no self in her; only a Presence like the red-gold sunlight and warm wind that filled the room. To kneel to this girl in this room seemed even familiar. It was like kneeling to the sea wind, or to a sudden vision of snow on the mountains, or to . . . supreme eloquence in music.[14]

Later that afternoon I went for a walk in the rain. As I walked I felt my body become peaceful. The gray of the landscape now seemed sweet and gentle, like old Chinese silk. I entered lovingly into the gray mist, the mud, the rain pouring down. The cold wind blowing into my face, which half an hour ago would have made me flinch and grit my teeth, became an exotic luxury, a sensation to be savored.

Then briefly I saw it. All the trees and fields were giving off white light, the light I had seen at *darshan,* that streamed from her photograph.

I was beginning to see reality consciously as divine, as an emanation of light . . . .[15]

◆

From Reshad Feild's *The Last Barrier: A Sufi Journey* comes this vivid description of a quiet moment of awakening visited upon the author while being instructed in breathing exercises by Hamid, a Sufi master:

As I relaxed, and allowed my body to breathe as Hamid directed, I felt an ease, a new sense of freedom that I had not experienced before. At the same time I had to struggle not to lose concentration and awareness....

"Now I want you to take several very deep breaths. Each time you breathe in, consciously attune yourself to be in balance, and at the same time take responsibility for your body. You have managed to let go of a lot of what you thought you were in order to discover something real in yourself. This is what we call the observer. You must learn to develop this observer a little more each day. You are here to learn to be in charge of the vehicle you have been given. Stand proud in this world, but bow in the next."

I breathed slowly and deeply.... The room looked quite different, as though I were seeing it for the first time. I felt a tremendous sense of peace and security. All was in its proper order. I sensed a perfect flow between the objects in the room, and through each object itself. There was a sense of communion, of acknowledgment—the chairs, the table, the bed, all knew of each other. They were not inanimate objects any more, but part of living Being. Everything had awareness, spoke a silent language. Everything was, in Essence, perfect.[16]

◆

Ram Dass, formerly Richard Alpert, has for thirty years been one of the West's most articulate seekers and teachers. In this passage from his insightful *Journey of Awakening: A Meditator's Guidebook*, he warns of the danger of clinging to any experience, including a transformative one:

I remember taking a fifteen-day insight meditation course. On the twelfth day, I experienced a peace that I had never known in my life. It was so deep that I rushed to my teacher and said, "This peace is what I have always wanted all my life. Everything else I was doing was just to find this peace." Yet a month later I was off pursuing other spiritual practices. That experience of peace wasn't enough. It was limited. Any experiential state, anything we can label, isn't it.

My intense experiences with psychedelics led to very powerful attachments to the memories of those trips. I tried to recreate them through yogic practices. It took some years before I stopped comparing meditative spaces with those of my psychedelic days. Only when I stopped clinging to those past experiences did I see that the present ones had a full-ness, immediacy, and richness that was enough—I didn't need the memories. Later, during intensive study of *pranayama* and *kundalini,* my breath stopped and I felt mo-ments of great rapture. Once again, the intensity of the ex-perience hooked me and I was held back for a time by my attempts to recreate those moments. When I saw that I was closest to God in the moment itself, these past experiences stopped having such a great pull. Again I saw my clinging to memories as an obstacle.[17]

◆

As a youth, Petaga, a Sioux medicine man, took part in the vision quest ceremony known as the Pipe Fast. Here, as told to fellow Sioux Arthur Amiotte and published in *I Be-come Part of It: Sacred Dimensions in Native American Life,* is part of Petaga's moving description of what he experienced during and after the Pipe Fast:

I stood alone with the cool breeze gently blowing. I could not tell from what direction. A warm sense of well-being came over me, and a comfort in my solitude welled up from within. . . . I was alone and quiet, naked before creation. Catches' words spoken in the sweat lodge floated through my consciousness: "He comes to you young and innocent. Have mercy on him and give him what he seeks." Indeed I felt as though I were newly born. . . .

As the sun traveled across the sky that day, the wonder of creation entered my awareness, the relation of microcosm and macrocosm; and I felt the connectedness of everything, as Catches had said, like a massive design woven by a sacred power, constantly breathed into by the breath of the Great Spirit. . . .

Later [after Petaga had returned from the wilderness] the people began to leave, to return that night for the final ceremony. . . . And I went out and sat on a stump by the woodpile and thought, and thought, and thought: how wonderful it was to be alive in this century yet also to experience the sacred traditions from the past and to know that the Great Spirit still responds to his twentieth-century children by giving them visions and signs and a sense of peace, and the knowledge of an all-enduring faith.[18]

NOTES

TRACY'S STORY

1. Quoted in Richard Maurice Bucke, *Cosmic Consciousness* (New York: E. P. Dutton, 1923), p. 274.

2. J. Krishnamurti, *The Awakening of Intelligence* (New York: Avon Books, 1973), p. 198.

3. William Segal, *The Middle Ground* (Brattleboro, VT: Stillgate Publishers, 1985).

DEATH

1. This and all biblical quotations are from the King James version of the Bible.

2. G. I. Gurdjieff, *Beelzebub's Tales to His Grandson, Third Book* (New York: E. P. Dutton, 1973), p. 373.

3. Quoted in Geir Kjetsaa, *Fyodor Dostoyevsky: A Writer's Life* (New York: Viking Penguin, 1987), p. 90.

4. Shantideva, *A Guide to the Bodhisattva's Way of Life,* quoted in Tenzin Gyatso, the Fourteenth Dalai Lama, *A Flash of Lightning in the Dark of Night,* trans. The Padmakara Translation Group (Boston: Shambhala Publications, 1994), p. 77.

LOVE

1. Jelaluddin Rumi, *Divani Shamsi Tabriz,* ed. and trans. R. A. Nicholson (Cambridge, 1898), p. 125.

2. James T. Boulton, ed., *The Letters of D. H. Lawrence, Vol. 1* (Cambridge: Cambridge University Press, 1979).

3. Leo Tolstoy, *War and Peace,* quoted in Robert Andrews, *The Columbia Dictionary of Quotations* (New York: Columbia University Press, 1979).

4. Brian Swimme, *The Universe Is a Green Dragon: A Cosmic Creation Story* (Santa Fe, NM: Bear and Company, 1984), p. 48.

5. Ibid., p. 48.

6. James Joyce, *A Portrait of the Artist as a Young Man* (New York: Penguin Books, 1985), pp. 171–72.

7. D. H. Lawrence, *Lady Chatterley's Lover* (New York: Bantam Books, 1983).

8. Julian of Norwich, *The Revelations of Divine Love of Julian of Norwich,* trans. James Walsh, S.J. (St. Meinrad, IN: Abbey Press, 1961), p. 120.

9. Eugene T. Gendlin, Ph.D., *Focusing* (New York: Bantam Books, 1981), p. 77.

10. Rainer Maria Rilke, *Letters to a Young Poet,* trans. Stephen Mitchell (Boston: Shambhala Publications, 1993), p. 81.

11. Bentley Layton, *The Gnostic Scriptures* (Garden City, NY: Doubleday and Company, 1987), p. 380.

12. *The Enlightened Mind: An Anthology of Sacred Prose,* ed. by Stephen Mitchell (New York: HarperCollins, 1991), p. 30.

NATURE

1. This distinction between essence and personality is drawn from the ideas of G. I. Gurdjieff.

2. Quoted in C. S. Nott, *Teachings of Gurdjieff: A Pupil's Journal* (London: Arkana, 1990), p. 168.

CREATIVITY

1. Rainer Maria Rilke, *Letters to A Young Poet,* trans. Stephen Mitchell (Boston: Shambhala Publications, 1993), p. 40.

2. From S. Sitwell, *Mozart* (New York: Appleton-Century-Crofts, 1932), quoted in Howard Gardner, *The Arts and Human Development* (New York: Basic Books, 1994), p. 268.

3. William James, *The Varieties of Religious Experience* (New York: Penguin Books, 1986).

4. Paul Davies, *The Mind of God* (New York: Simon & Schuster, 1982), p. 228.

5. Fred Hoyle, "The Universe: Past and Present Reflections," University of Cardiff report 70 (1981), quoted in Davies, *Mind of God,* pp. 228–29.

6. Quoted in an advertisement for The New School, *The New York Times,* January 13, 1995.

CYBERSPACE

1. John Perry Barlow, "Being in Nothingness," *Microtimes Magazine,* February 1990.

2. Tracy Cochran, "Samsara Squared," *Tricycle: The Buddhist Review,* Fall 1992.

3. Jaron Lanier, interviewed by Maria Wilhelm, "Comparative Illusions," *Tricycle: The Buddhist Review,* Summer 1994.

4. Cochran, "Samsara Squared."

5. John Perry Barlow, "Is There a There in Cyberspace?" *Utne Reader,* March–April 1995.

SCIENCE

1. Francis Crick, *The Astonishing Hypothesis: The Scientific Search for the Soul* (New York: Charles Scribner's Sons, 1994), p. 3.

2. Ibid., p. 259.

3. Ibid., p. 7.

4. Richard Dawkins, *The Selfish Gene* (Oxford: Oxford University Press, 1976).

5. Ibid.

6. Crick, *The Astonishing Hypothesis,* p. 258.

7. Ibid., p. 268.

8. Larry Dossey, M.D. *Recovering the Soul: A Scientific and Spiritual Search* (New York: Bantam Books, 1989), p. 197.

9. Jeremy Hayward and Francisco J. Varela, eds., *Gentle Bridges: Conversations with the Dalai Lama on the Sciences of Mind* (Boston: Shambhala Publications, 1992), p. 153.

10. Quoted in Perle Epstein, *Kabbalah: The Way of the Jewish Mystic* (Boston: Shambhala Publications, 1978), p. 87.

11. Peter Fenwick, "Meditation, Altered States and the Mind/Body Relationship," *The Bridge,* #10 (1994), pp. 39–40.

12. Larry Dossey, *Healing Words* (San Francisco: HarperSanFrancisco, 1993), p. 16.

13. Ibid., p. 18.

14. Hayward and Varela, *Gentle Bridges,* p. 187.

15. Ibid., p. 186.

16. Daniel Goleman, "New Kind of Memory Found to Preserve Moments of Emotion," *The New York Times,* October 25, 1994.

17. From "Collected Sayings" of the Maggid of Mezerich, trans. Aryeh Kaplan, quoted in Aryeh Kaplan, "Sparks in the Night," an unpublished manuscript quoted in Epstein, *Kabbalah,* p. 116.

SURRENDER

1. Donald Newlove, *Those Drinking Days* (New York: McGraw-Hill Book Company, 1988), pp. 65–67.

2. Ibid., pp. 102–103.

3. Ibid., p. 107.

4. Ibid., p. 109.

TRADITIONS

1. *Bhagavad Gita,* Chapter 11, trans. Sir Edwin Arnold, quoted in *A Treasury of Asian Literature,* ed. John D. Yohannan (New York: New American Library, 1984), p. 368.

A PARTING THOUGHT

1. Meister Eckhart, quoted in William Segal, *Opening* (Sunderland, MA: Green River Press, 1993), p. 2.

TRANSFORMING MOMENTS

1. Claire Booth Luce, quoted in *The Road to Damascus: The Spiritual Pilgrimage of Fifteen Converts to Catholicism,* ed. John A. O'Brien (Garden City, NY: Doubleday, 1949), pp. 223–24.

2. Bill Wilson, quoted in Andrew Delbanco and Thomas Delbanco, "A.A. at the Crossroads," *The New Yorker,* March 20, 1995, p. 52.

3. David Chadwick, *Thank You and OK!: An American Zen Failure in Japan* (New York: Penguin/Arkana, 1994), p. 195.

4. Charles G. Finney, *Memoirs of Rev. Charles G. Finney* (New York: 1876).

5. Rachel Cowan, quoted in Joshua O. Haberman, *The God I Believe In* (New York: The Free Press, 1994), p. 27–28.

6. Paul Brunton, quoted in Kenneth Thurston Hurst, *Paul Brunton: A Personal View* (Burdett, NY: Larson Publications, 1989).

7. C. S. Lewis, *Surprised by Joy* (New York: Harcourt Brace & Co., 1955).

8. Gavin Harrison, *In the Lap of the Buddha* (Boston: Shambhala Publications, 1994), pp. 15–16.

9. Vivekananda, quoted in Christopher Isherwood, *The Wishing Tree* (San Francisco. Harper & Row, 1987), p. 117.

10. Charles Tart, *Open Mind, Discriminating Mind: Reflections on Human Possibilities* (New York: Harper & Row, 1989), p. 272–73.

11. St. Augustine, *Confessions,* trans. E. B. Pusey (London: J. M. Dent & Sons, 1966), pp. 170–71.

12. Caitlin O'Sullivan, quoted in Rabbi Daniel B. Syme, *Why I Am a Reform Jew* (New York: Donald I. Fine, Inc., 1989), p. 208.

13. Helen Keller, *Hellen Keller: The Story of My Life* (New York: Signet/New American Library, 1988), p. 18.

14. Andrew Harvey, *Hidden Journey: A Spiritual Awakening* (New York: Penguin/Arkana, 1992), p. 33.

15. Ibid., p. 204.

16. Reshad Feild, *The Last Barrier: A Sufi Journey* (Rockport, MA: Element, 1993), p. 36.

17. Ram Dass, *Journey of Awakening: A Meditator's Guidebook* (New York: Bantam, 1990), p. 147

18. Petaga, quoted in Arthur Amiotte, "Eagles Fly Over," in *I Become Part of It: Sacred Dimensions in Native American Life,* ed. D. M. Dooling and Paul Jordan-Smith (New York: Parabola Books, 1989), pp. 215, 218–19, 231–32.

ABOUT THE AUTHORS

Tracy Cochran is a consulting editor to *Tricycle: The Buddhist Review*. She has written for *The New York Times, The Sunday Boston Globe, Omni* magazine, *New York* magazine, and other publications, and is the author of a young adult adventure novel. Her husband, Jeff Zaleski, is also a consulting editor to *Tricycle: The Buddhist Review*. Formerly the executive director of *Parabola* magazine and the nonfiction editor of *Kirkus Reviews*, he is now a contributing editor to *Publishers Weekly* and writes for a variety of publications. Tracy and Jeff, both of whom are twins, live in Brooklyn with their daughter, Alexandra.

Marc David
NOURISHING WISDOM
A Mind/Body Approach to Nutrition and Well-Being
A book that advocates awareness in eating.
0-517-88129-2 Softcover

◆

Kat Duff
THE ALCHEMY OF ILLNESS
A luminous inquiry into the function and purpose of illness.
0-517-88097-0 Softcover

◆

Noela N. Evans
MEDITATIONS FOR THE PASSAGES
AND CELEBRATIONS OF LIFE
A Book of Vigils
Articulating the often unspoken emotions experienced
at such times as birth, death, and marriage.
0-517-59341-6 Hardcover
0-517-88299-X Softcover

◆

Burghild Nina Holzer
A WALK BETWEEN HEAVEN AND EARTH
A Personal Journal on Writing and the Creative Process
How keeping a journal focuses and expands our awareness
of ourselves and everything that touches our lives.
0-517-88096-2 Softcover

◆

Greg Johanson and Ron Kurtz
GRACE UNFOLDING
Psychotherapy in the Spirit of the Tao-te ching
The interaction of client and therapist illuminated through the
gentle power and wisdom of Lao Tsu's ancient Chinese classic.
0-517-88130-6 Softcover

◆

Selected by Marcia and Jack Kelly
ONE HUNDRED GRACES
Mealtime Blessings
A collection of graces from many traditions, inscribed in
calligraphy reminiscent of the manuscripts of medieval Europe.
0-517-58567-7 Hardcover
0-517-88230-2 Softcover

Jack and Marcia Kelly
SANCTUARIES
A Guide to Lodgings in Monasteries, Abbeys, and
Retreats of the United States
For those in search of renewal and a little peace; described by
The New York Times as "the *Michelin Guide* of the retreat set."
THE NORTHEAST *0-517-57727-5 Softcover*
WEST COAST & SOUTHWEST *0-517-88007-5 Softcover*

◆

Barbara Lachman
THE JOURNAL OF HILDEGARD OF BINGEN
A year in the life of the twelfth-century German saint—
the diary she never had the time to write herself.
0-517-59169-3 Hardcover
0-517-88390-2 Softcover

◆

Katherine Le Mée
CHANT
The Origins, Form, Practice, and Healing Power
of Gregorian Chant
The ways in which this ancient liturgy
can nourish us and transform our lives.
0-517-70037-9 Hardcover

◆

Gunilla Norris
BECOMING BREAD
Meditations on Loving and Transformation
A book linking the food of the spirit—love—
with the food of the body—bread.
0-517-59168-5 Hardcover

BEING HOME
A Book of Meditations
An exquisite modern book of hours,
a celebration of mindfulness in everyday activities.
0-517-58159-0 Hardcover

JOURNEYING IN PLACE
Reflections from a Country Garden
Another classic book of meditations
illuminating the sacredness of daily experience.
0-517-59762-4 Hardcover

SHARING SILENCE
Meditation Practice and Mindful Living
A book describing the essential conditions
for meditating in a group or on one's own.
0-517-59506-0 Hardcover

◆

Ram Dass and Mirabai Bush
COMPASSION IN ACTION
Setting Out on the Path of Service
Heartfelt encouragement and advice for those ready
to commit time and energy to relieving suffering in the world.
0-517-88500-X Softcover

◆

Rabbi Rami M. Shapiro
WISDOM OF THE JEWISH SAGES
A Modern Reading of **Pirke Avot**
A third-century treasury of maxims on justice, integrity, and
virtue—Judaism's principal ethical scripture.
0-517-79966-9 Hardcover

———◆———

Richard Whelan
SELF-RELIANCE
The Wisdom of Ralph Waldo Emerson
as Inspiration for Daily Living
A distillation of Emerson's spiritual writings
for contemporary readers.
0-517-58512-X Softcover

Bell Tower books are for sale at your local bookstore or you may call
Random House at 1-800-793-BOOK to order with a credit card.